DAVID WALKER

THE
TRANSPARENT
LYRIC

Reading and Meaning in the
Poetry of Stevens and Williams

Princeton University Press

for my parents

Contents

Books are to be call'd for, and supplied, on the assumption that the process of reading is not a half-sleep, but, in the highest sense, an exercise, a gymnast's struggle; that the reader is to do something for himself, must be on the alert, must himself or herself construct indeed the poem, argument, history, metaphysical essay—the text furnishing the hints, the clue, the start or frame-work. Not the book needs so much to be the complete thing, but the reader of the book does. That were to make a nation of supple and athletic minds, well-train'd, intuitive, used to depend on themselves, and not on a few coteries of writers.

Walt Whitman, "Democratic Vistas"

Preface

This study suggests readings of a number of poems by Wallace
Stevens and William Carlos Williams within the broader con-
text of an investigation of a modern lyric genre. It had its
beginnings in general reservations about some of the existing
criticism of the two poets. I was puzzled first by the persistent
attempt by many historical and theoretical critics alike to treat
Stevens and Williams as polar opposites—reductively, the poet
of "the poem of the act of the mind" and the poet of "no
ideas but in things"—and to minimize what I saw as important
formal and thematic similarities. More specifically, I was per-
plexed by the frequent misreadings—as they seemed to me—
of Stevens' tone, by the confusing discussions of Williams'
Objectivism, and by apparent contradictions in treatments of
each poet's "impersonality." Armed with no more theoretical
ammunition than what I hoped were imagination and com-
mon sense, I intended to set forth my own conclusions on
these and other matters.

As my work progressed, I began to realize that my differ-
ences with other critics were not simple matters of interpre-
tation, but were based on profoundly different assumptions
about what the experience of reading the poems of Stevens
and Williams entailed. Indeed, the poems I wanted to discuss
seemed to exemplify a development in modern literature to
which criticism had not adequately responded. Let me cite a
couple of examples. In *The Possibility of Criticism*, Monroe C.
Beardsley says the following:

> Three fundamental and universal things can be said about
> poems: first, that every poem has an implicit *dramatic
> speaker*, whose words are the words we read or hear;
> second, that every dramatic speaker is confronted with
> some kind of *situation*, however broadly described; and

third, that one of the fundamental axes on which the
poem turns is the speaker's *attitude* toward that situa-
tion—how he purports to feel about it, his emotions and
reflective thoughts.[1]

These ideas about the kinds of speech acts represented by
poetry have been refined and extended in various ways, but
the influence of the New Criticism continues to make itself
felt. The metaphors of dramatic speaker and voice are used
universally, without enough attention to the assumptions on
which such terminology rests. Here, for instance, is the be-
ginning of one of Stevens' poems, "A Golden Woman in a
Silver Mirror":

> Suppose this was the root of everything.
> Suppose it turned out to be or that it touched
> An image that was mistress of the world.
>
> For example: Au Château. Un Salon. A glass
> The sun steps into, regards and finds itself;
> Or: Gawks of hay . . . Augusta Moon, before
>
> An attic glass, hums of the old Lutheran bells
> At home; or: In the woods, belle Belle alone
> Rattles with fear in unreflecting leaves.[2]

To argue that we are intended to be conscious of these words
as uttered by a speaker dramatized in a particular situation,
and further that one of the cruxes of our reading experience
is that speaker's attitude toward his or her situation, is to
inhibit our approach to the poem. The notion of the dramatic
speaker is a fundamentally realistic one, since it depends on
conventions of consistency and identity, whereas this passage
uses discontinuity, fantastic inversions, and self-parody to de-
molish the illusion that it is spoken by a concretely realized
character in any situation we can imagine. The poem works
not by dramatizing character but, like many other Stevens
poems, by the lyrical and dialectical projection of idea. What
purports to be a straightforward list of examples of the image

in the title turns out to be itself a wilderness of mirrors: in a series of theatrical tableaux, the reflected sun is reflected by Augusta Moon, whose remembered bells are in turn mirrored by belle Belle, who is not mirrored by the "unreflecting leaves" that surround her, but whose name itself provides a kind of mirror image. The meaning of the poem rests in the ways we find to acknowledge and make sense of such gestures (and others: the verbal extravagance of "gawks of hay," the fact that "The Old Lutheran Bells at Home" is the title of another Stevens poem, and so on). As the following chapters demonstrate, the dramatic center of such poems is not a lyric speaker but the reading experience itself.

More recently, in his illuminating *Making Sense of Literature* John Reichert writes, "The reading of all imaginative literature depends [on] imagining a personality behind the words spoken and the deed performed. We read the words and think of the deeds *as if* there were a Hamlet who speaks and acts, a Pip who recounts his past to us."[3] No doubt this is exactly what happens in *Hamlet* and *Great Expectations*, but it is not necessarily true of all imaginative literature. Reichert continues by quoting Pound's "In a Station of the Metro" and then commenting (p. 18):

> Part of our understanding of this poem has to do with seeing how the two lines are related to each other. And one way to get at the relationship is to ask in what sort of actual situation two such phrases might be spoken in conjunction with each other. What kind of utterance is it?

This may be a productive way to approach Pound's poem, but it is precisely the wrong question to ask about Williams' "The Locust Tree in Flower":

> Among
> of
> green

stiff
old
bright

broken
branch
come

white
sweet
May

again[4]

This poem simply cannot be understood as the utterance of any dramatized speaker in any actual situation. Its meaning inheres not in any externally projected drama, but in the drama of sensibility that is enacted as one reads it. I propose to call this kind of poem the transparent lyric: in replacing the lyric speaker with the reader as the center of dramatic attention, the poem itself becomes a transparent medium through which the reader is led to see the world in a particular way. If my analysis is correct, this calls into question many of our traditional assumptions about lyric speakers, personas, and situations.

"A Golden Woman in a Silver Mirror" and "The Locust Tree in Flower" are more disjunctive in their surfaces and disruptive of the notion of dramatic presence than much of the other work of Stevens and Williams. Many of their poems may be seen to fall squarely into the traditions of dramatic monologue and dramatic lyric. But the tendency to use the rhetoric of the poem—even one with an apparently more consecutive surface—to shift the dramatic center from a lyric speaker to the reading experience itself, is strong throughout the career of each poet. Not every poem by Stevens and Williams is a transparent lyric, but the quality of transparence and the rhetorical strategies through which it is achieved represent crucial aspects of the value and meaning of their work.

To an extent, of course, the meaning of all literature de-

pends on the interaction between text and reader. As Wolf-
gang Iser says of reading in general, "The work is more than
the text, for the text only takes on life when it is realized, and
furthermore the realization is by no means independent of the
individual disposition of the reader. . . . The convergence of
text and reader brings the literary work into existence."⁵ Yet
I begin with the assumptions that the dynamics of this inter-
action vary from text to text, that the meaning of some texts
may be said to be more fully defined or determined within
the text than the meaning of others, and that much of modern
literary history may be understood in terms of the shifting
relationship between meaning and the act of reading. Susan
Suleiman has pointed out that Iser's position on the nature of
the relationship between text and reader is ambiguous: he both
asserts the primacy of the reader's creative role and suggests
that ultimately it is the text itself that directs the reader's
realization of it.⁶ The question of the relative determinacy and
indeterminacy of texts, of the interdependent roles of text and
reader in the alchemy of meaning, is enormously complex
and finally mysterious, and I cannot hope to resolve it. But
particularly since reader-response criticism has tended to focus
either on prose fiction or on poetry governed by the conven-
tions of dramatic speaker and situation, it seems especially
important to explore the demands made on the reader of the
lyric poetry I call transparent.

These issues will be developed in detail in the chapters that
follow, but I want to emphasize two points here. The first is
that this book is not intended as a comprehensive study of
the work of Stevens and Williams; many of the major thematic
concerns of each poet, and many of their most important
poems, are not mentioned. For more generalized discussion,
I can simply recommend such studies as those by Frank Ker-
mode, Joseph Riddel, and Harold Bloom on Stevens, and by
James Guimond, Thomas Whitaker, and James Breslin on
Williams. My purpose here is narrower: I want to demonstrate
the importance of a distinctive lyric form by examining its
centrality in the work of two distinguished modern poets.

And because any literary theory is only as valuable as the insights it yields into individual texts, I hope to show that the idea of transparence enables us to read the poems of Stevens and Williams with greater insight and accuracy.

My other point of emphasis, perhaps clear from what I have already said, is that my chief approach throughout is not thematic but rhetorical and epistemological. Like other recent critics, I intend to explore the relation of Stevens and Williams to the literary tradition. But whereas thematic concerns have led many to conclude that the two poets remain essentially Romantic, my emphasis on rhetorical and dramatic strategy suggests some crucial differences from Romanticism and even from High Modernism. To take one example, George Bornstein describes cogently the ways in which a poem like "The Idea of Order at Key West" diverges from the Romantic paradigms, and his discussion of "double consciousness" and the ironic, "self-canceling" voice of Stevens' late poems anticipates my own; yet his thematic emphasis causes him to see Stevens as a new, "transformed" Romantic, whereas my focus on the role of the reader elicits some differences that seem to me essential.[7] Ultimately, the issue of determining whether or not Stevens and Williams should be categorized as Romantics is less important than the question of what their poems mean, and how they achieve meaning. Critics less subtle than Bornstein have taken the presumed Romanticism of the two poets as license for subjecting their work to the excesses of expressivist analysis, and it is to this tendency that I want primarily to respond. My own conclusion is that the transparent lyric of Stevens and Williams represents a bridge between the earlier, essentially Symbolist poetics of Yeats and Eliot and the tradition that Marjorie Perloff has defined as "the poetics of indeterminacy";[8] the chapters that follow are meant to suggest why.

This book is intended to demonstrate the degree to which the transparent lyric is a characteristic and important form in the work of Stevens and Williams, the variety and range of uses to which each poet put it, the gains in understanding that may be reached by considering these poems in terms of their transparence, and the aesthetic and philosophical implications of such consideration. In pursuing these various ends, I have chosen to organize the book as a series of essays on related topics rather than as a single evolving argument. The first chapter defines the transparent lyric in terms of its historical and cultural context, and then introduces the study of Stevens' use of the form through discussion of three examples. The second chapter explores the relationship between reading and meaning defined in many of Stevens' poems through the metaphors of the theater and the book. Chapter Three emphasizes the ways in which the rhetoric of the transparent lyric leads to active engagement between the reader and the poem, by demonstrating Stevens' dynamic treatment of the process of metaphorical thinking; and Chapter Four argues the particular importance of recognizing the quality of transparence in his late poems. In the fifth chapter I provide a transition to Williams by examining his personal and aesthetic relationship to Stevens, and then go on to illustrate the significance of transparence in the development of his wide-ranging career, particularly in its relation to the Objectivist movement. The final chapter suggests that in his work following *Paterson*, Williams used the rhetoric of the transparent lyric to balance the personal voice and vision more often recognized as characteristic of this phase, thus producing some of his most original achievements. The book concludes with a postscript that suggests the importance of the rhetoric and epistemology of the transparent lyric to the generation of poets that followed Stevens and Williams.

I want to express my gratitude to a number of friends and colleagues for providing valuable advice and encouragement, especially Ann Boehm, Stephen Fix, Deborah Lubar, James McConkey, James Merod, Anne Posel, Daniel Schwarz, Walter Slatoff, and Carol Tufts. Thanks are also due to the Oberlin students who have taught me much while studying these poets with me. I am grateful to Robert Buttel, Jack Stillinger, and Thomas Whitaker, who read the manuscript and offered helpful suggestions, and to Marjorie Sherwood and Margaret Case of Princeton University Press. My greatest debt is to David Young, for his teaching, his generosity, and his constant example.

Oberlin
August 1983

Acknowledgments

Two short passages from this book first appeared in *Field: Contemporary Poetry and Poetics*, and are reprinted by permission.

Grateful acknowledgment is made to the following for permission to reprint copyrighted material:

Alfred A. Knopf, Inc., and Faber & Faber, Ltd., for permission to quote from the copyrighted works of Wallace Stevens.

New Directions Publishing Corporation, for permission to quote from the following works by William Carlos Williams: *Autobiography of William Carlos Williams*, copyright 1951 by William Carlos Williams; *Collected Earlier Poems*, copyright 1938 by New Directions Publishing Corporation; *Imaginations*, copyright © 1923, 1931, 1938, 1951, 1957 by William Carlos Williams; *In the American Grain*, copyright 1925 by James Laughlin, 1933 by William Carlos Williams; *Many Loves & Other Plays*, copyright 1936, 1942, 1948 by William Carlos Williams, © 1961 by Florence H. Williams; *Pictures from Breughel and Other Poems*, copyright © 1949, 1951, 1952, 1953, 1954, 1955, 1956, 1957, 1959, 1960, 1961, 1962 by William Carlos Williams; *Selected Essays*, copyright 1954 by William Carlos Williams; *Selected Letters*, copyright 1957 by William Carlos Williams.

New Directions Publishing Corporation and Faber & Faber, Ltd., for permission to quote from *Personae* by Ezra Pound, copyright 1926 by Ezra Pound.

Viking Penguin, Inc., for permission to quote from *Houseboat Days* by John Ashbery, copyright © 1975, 1976, 1977 by John Ashbery.

Abbreviations

The following editions are used throughout, abbreviated as indicated:

By Wallace Stevens:

CP   *Collected Poems* (New York: Knopf, 1954)
L   *Letters*, ed. Holly Stevens (New York: Knopf, 1966)
NA   *The Necessary Angel: Essays on Reality and the Imagination* (New York: Knopf, 1951)
OP   *Opus Posthumous*, ed. Samuel French Morse (New York: Knopf, 1957)

By William Carlos Williams:

A   *Autobiography* (New York: Random House, 1951)
CEP   *Collected Earlier Poems* (New York: New Directions, 1951)
CLP   *Collected Later Poems* (New York: New Directions, 1963)
I   *Imaginations*, ed. Webster Schott (New York: New Directions, 1970)
IAG   *In the American Grain* (New York: New Directions, 1956)
ML   *Many Loves and Other Plays* (New York: New Directions, 1961)
P   *Paterson* (New York: New Directions, 1963)
PB   *Pictures from Breughel* (New York: New Directions, 1962)
SE   *Selected Essays* (New York: Random House, 1954)
SL   *Selected Letters*, ed. John C. Thirlwall (New York: McDowell, Obolensky, 1957)

THE
TRANSPARENT
LYRIC

1

The Transparent Lyric

I seem'd about this period to have sight
Of a new world, a world too, that was fit
To be transmitted and made visible
To other eyes, as having for its base
That whence our dignity originates,
That which both gives it being and maintains
A balance, an ennobling interchange
Of action from within and from without,
The excellence, pure spirit, and best power
Both of the object seen, and eye that sees.

Wordsworth, *The Prelude*

　　　. . . Description is
Composed of a sight indifferent to the eye.

It is an expectation, a desire,
A palm that rises up beyond the sea,

A little different from reality:
The difference that we make in what we see

And our memorials of that difference,
Sprinklings of bright particulars from the sky.

Stevens, "Description Without Place"

The inevitable flux of the seeing eye toward measuring itself
by the world it inhabits can only result in . . . crushing hu-
miliation unless the individual rise to some appropriate co-
extension with the universe. This is possible by aid of the
imagination.

Williams, *Spring and All*

> It was not so much the lost terrestrial,
> The snug hibernal from that sea and salt,
> That century of wind in a single puff.
> What counted was mythology of self,
> Blotched out beyond unblotching. . . .
> Crispin was washed away by magnitude,
> The whole of life that still remained in him
> Dwindled to one sound strumming in his ear,
> Ubiquitous concussion, slap and sigh,
> Polyphony beyond his baton's thrust.

Wallace Stevens' early mock-epic, "The Comedian as the Letter C" (CP, 27-46), is a parable of the modern self, tracing through the adventures of its "minuscule" hero a central fact of modern intellectual experience. Setting out from his comfortable eighteenth-century world "of simple salad-beds, / Of honest quilts" for an ocean voyage to Yucatan, Havana, and Carolina, Crispin is shocked into a crisis of identity by the sheer power and magnitude of the sea. His "eye of land" no longer suffices in this "inscrutable world," where all of nature is reduced to the mindless, uncontrollable "slap and sigh" of waves. The apparent hostility of the landscape shatters his complacent convictions:

> The salt hung on his spirit like a frost,
> The dead brine melted in him like a dew
> Of winter, until nothing of himself
> Remained, except some starker, barer self
> In a starker, barer world. . . .
>   . . . Crispin
> Became an introspective voyager.

The history of modern thought and art may be read as a series of such introspective voyages—with widely divergent destinations, certainly, but originating in essentially the same disturbing confrontation between the self and an alien world.

    This sense of disjuncture had its roots in the emphasis of

such diverse thinkers as Augustine, Luther, and Descartes on the subjective freedom of the ego, and developed into the radical individualism of the Romantic period. The general world view that emerged among the important philosophers of mind and art at the beginning of the nineteenth century was potentially bleak and dangerous. According to the English empiricists, nature was mechanical and empty, all *a priori* knowledge was suspect, and man's understanding of the world was confined to the limited light he could cast on it. In his account of the sources and development of Romantic theory, M. H. Abrams emphasizes the powerful impact of the ethical system of Kant,

> with its basic concept of man "as belonging to two worlds"—the noumenal and phenomenal worlds—and its consequent view that to be civilized involves a continuous tension, which can never be completely resolved, between the categorical demands of the noumenal ego, or moral will, which assumes absolute freedom, and the inescapable limitations of the phenomenal ego, or man as a part of nature, and therefore subject both to his instinctual and sensual drives and to the laws of strict causal necessity.[1]

The naturalization of the universe, and the consciousness of man's ontological separation from it, helped to provoke the familiar Romantic appeal to the organic faculty of imagination. Through the power of imaginative vision, man could hope to bridge the gap between subject and object, to restore a vital, significant relationship between the self and nature, and to rediscover meaning in a fragmented universe. In an act of sympathetic intuition, the imagination could identify itself with its object, and in that moment of direct perception could effect a bond between the self and the external world.

A corollary of the Romantic emphasis on the shaping spirit of the imagination is the view of nature as symbolic. Blake's conviction that the phenomenal world was corrupt and deceptive, and that the task of the visionary eye was to penetrate

to the spiritual truth that natural objects concealed, is only an
extreme version of a general Romantic tendency. "I always
seek in what I see," Shelley said, "the likeness of something
beyond the present and tangible object."[2] The positions of
both Wordsworth and Coleridge were considerably more di-
vided, emphasizing the concrete, vital reality of phenomenal
nature, and at the same time attempting to sustain a vision of
transcendental order as revealed by the natural world. The
role of the imagination, according to Coleridge's "Dynamic
Philosophy," was to merge the worlds of objects and of forms,
the real and the ideal, in a moment of resonant, generative
perception. And the purpose of art was in turn to capture that
moment of synthesis in a form which represented both fact
and vision; as Coleridge said in his lecture, "On Poesy or
Art,"

> Art itself might be defined as of a middle quality between
> a thought and a thing, or . . . the union and reconcili-
> ation of that which is nature with that which is exclu-
> sively human. It is the figured language of thought, and
> is distinguished from nature by the unity of all the parts
> in one thought or idea. . . . To make the external in-
> ternal, the internal external, to make nature thought,
> and thought nature,—this is the mystery of genius in
> the Fine Arts.[3]

The goal of Romantic poetry as expressed by Coleridge, then,
may be seen as a kind of unifying vision, moving both sym-
pathetically outward toward the object and self-consciously
inward, in order to reveal the truth of subjective vision with-
out distorting the evidence of the objective world.

But poetry so dependent on individual perception always
runs the risk of some distortion, of swinging toward the pole
of absolute subjectivity. Although the value of their art de-
pended on the authenticity of personal vision, the Romantics
persistently sought ways to escape the obsessive threat of
solipsism. The tension that inevitably resulted is seen clearly
in the case of Keats, the Romantic poet most deeply concerned

with transcending the boundaries of individual consciousness.
Keats believed his imagination capable of moving beyond
himself to ecstatic union with nature through the empathic
faculty of Negative Capability. Distinguishing himself from
"the wordsworthian or egotistical sublime," he relished his
"camelion" character:

> A poet is the most unpoetical of any thing in existence;
> because he has no Identity—he is continually in for—
> and filling some other Body—The Sun, the Moon, the
> Sea and Men and Women who are creatures of impulse
> are poetical and have about them an unchangeable at-
> tribute—the poet has none; no identity.[4]

This kind of imaginative projection may well have served in
his own experience of reverie to liberate Keats from egotism;
as he said, "if a Sparrow come before my Window I take part
in its existince and pick about the gravel."[5] Indeed, this sen-
sation of radical sympathy, or *Einfühlung*, is variously de-
scribed by all the Romantics.[6] But since writing is inevitably
a self-conscious action, to write a poem about such an ex-
perience is paradoxical. The subject of the "Ode to a Night-
ingale," for example, is the urge to be liberated from the self,
and to merge with the transcendental harmony and perfection
that the nightingale represents. Given the extraordinary power
of Keats' imagination, he may well have had the experience
of momentarily merging with the bird on that sunny morning
in 1819. But in writing a poem about the experience, no matter
how immediate and transparent his description, he paradox-
ically affirms the ultimate separation from the world implicit
in his act of consciousness. As Robert Pinsky notes, "the more
actively he pursues the natural world he loves, the more al-
ienated he is from it, for its attribute is not to enumerate.
Above all, the more he knows it or tries to perfect that knowl-
edge in his writing, the more he widens the gap between
himself and it, because its essence is not to be conscious at
all. In effect, it is this unconsciousness or 'pure' being which
he loves, and the more he knows and articulates the object of

his love, the less like it he is."[7] The process of organizing his experience into poetic form divides Keats from nature's blissful ignorance, and tolls him back to his sole self as unrelentingly as the word "forlorn."

This separation is further compounded by the act of reading the poem. The "I" whose voice we hear is recognizably different from ourselves, and the experience he describes remains emphatically his rather than ours. The reader of the poem— we might say of Romantic poems in general—occupies the same position as the reader of "Lycidas," spying from behind a tree while the shepherd laments the loss of his friend. The meaning and movement of the poem are controlled by the meditation of the lyric speaker. And though we are always required to engage the experience that the poem describes with our imaginations, and may often sympathize deeply with it, we inevitably remain observers, perceptibly distanced from the visionary moment toward which the poem moves.

The reader of the Romantic meditative lyric, then, is distanced from the phenomenal world of the poem, from the nature its lyric speaker encounters, in two distinct ways: by the poet's own self-consciousness, necessary to write the poem, and by the recognition that the poem reflects the experience of an identifiable discrete personality. The nightingale is perceived not directly but indirectly, at two removes, and the medium of the text serves not to project an ecstatic moment but to record an experience already achieved. For the reader, I would argue, the rhetorical stance of the poem effectively prevents that ideal merger of self and nature, of mind and object, that Coleridge compellingly described.

This separation is even more clear in "Tintern Abbey." The power of Wordsworth's poem is in its meditative movement, its drama of a mind confronting experience and attempting to reconcile the inner and outer landscapes. Yet despite the essentially restless, exploratory character of the poem, the reader is fundamentally excluded from its action except as sympathetic listener. The poem's subject is the struggle to redeem and recreate an active bond with the world of external nature, but its dialectic operates entirely between the poet and nature and does not require the reader's presence. The reader occupies a position strikingly analogous to that of the implied auditor in the poem, Wordsworth's sister, who is as passive as the poet is active. Dorothy exists in the poem primarily as an audience whom William can address, and onto whom he can project his fears and aspirations. She may sympathize deeply with his experience, but she does not share it—nor is she yet capable of doing so, as the poet makes clear:

> in thy voice I catch
> The language of my former heart, and read
> My former pleasures in the shooting lights
> Of thy wild eyes.

Wordsworth's attitude toward his sister and his reader is largely patronizing; he is "a man speaking to men," but from the distant heights to which his "more lively sensibility, more enthusiasm and tenderness" have led him. And indeed, it is difficult to see how poetry grounded in expressive theories of art could do other than gravitate toward the subjective pole. If nature is symbolic and requires interpretation, if it presents itself as a puzzle that, as Wordsworth says, "yields up" meaning, then the poet assumes a primary interpretive role that inherently assigns to readers a secondary one. Keats (in his letters), Wordsworth (in the Preface to *Lyrical Ballads*), and the other Romantics to a lesser extent all demonstrate that they are very much aware of the reader reading their poems. In *The Prelude* (V. 591-605) Wordsworth likens poetry to nature as material for the reader's imagination to work on. Nevertheless, "nature" in the poem remains essentially shaped and interpreted by the lyric speaker's meditation. The dramatic structure of the Romantic lyric thus mediates between the reader and the phenomenal world of the poem. In this sense, the ideal Romantic sensation of simultaneous sympathy and self-consciousness, of fusing noumenal and phenomenal worlds, is not one the rhetorical strategy of the Romantic poem invites the reader to share.

★

As such critics as Robert Langbaum, Frank Kermode, and
Harold Bloom have demonstrated, modern poets are clearly
the inheritors of the Romantics, in their concern with the
situation and process of the individual consciousness, and the
expression of consciousness in works of imagination.[8] The
New Critical insistence on a division between Romanticism
and Modernism has been widely displaced by the assumption
that twentieth-century poetry is an extension of the Romantic
tradition. But recent attempts to demonstrate that inheritance
have minimized some crucial distinctions. Though Stevens'
Crispin shares the Romantic crisis of alienation from the land-
scape, his response is essentially anti-Romantic:

> . . . Severance
> Was clear. The last distortion of romance
> Forsook the insatiable egotist. The sea
> Severs not only lands but also selves.
> Here was no help before reality.
> Crispin beheld and Crispin was made new.
> The imagination, here, could not evade,
> In poems of plums, the strict austerity
> Of one vast, subjugating, final tone.
>
> (CP, 30)

The Romantics' attempt to see beyond the disordered partic-
ulars of experience into a transcendent realm of unity and
wholeness is for modern poets in general an evasive and fal-
sifying impulse. Nature is no longer symbolic, but an irra-
tional and autonomous "other"; as Stevens says, we live "in
the world of Darwin and not in the world of Plato" (OP,
246). Stripped of the sanctions of Romantic idealism, the poet
can no longer assume any inherent reciprocity between imag-
ination and nature. Thus the other tenet of Romantic criti-
cism—confidence in the power of the imagination to create
harmonious bonds between self and world—also becomes
suspect. If reality is shifting and ephemeral, then any attempt

to establish a systematic communion with it is simply an egotistical projection and doomed to failure.

It may, of course, be argued that the notion of Romantic idealism is intensely problematic even among the High Romantics, that skepticism about the possibility of achieving a harmonious bond with the world of nature is very much a part of the poetry of Wordsworth and Keats. It may also be claimed that the reaction I have called anti-Romantic is simply a "swerving" firmly within the Romantic tradition.[9] I would suggest simply that transcendentalism remains a fundamental ideal for the High Romantics, however problematic, and that the science and the new philosophies of the late nineteenth and early twentieth centuries make the idealist solution considerably more difficult for most poets of this century to accept. Further, this shift in sensibility has profound consequences for the formal and rhetorical strategies of modern poetry. Despite the proliferation of studies of the relation of modernism to Romanticism, most have focused primarily on philosophical and thematic issues; by exploring structural and rhetorical considerations, I hope to demonstrate some important differences in the situation of the modern poets in terms of their complex relation to their world, their language, and their audience.

As the possibility of discovering order in the external world of nature grew more remote, modern poets turned increasingly with their questions of identity and continuity to the more coherent world of art. And given what they perceived as the limitations of the fixed, subjective voice of the Romantic poem, given the challenge to the coherence of mind and matter inherent in the threat of solipsism, they devoted particular attention to achieving a quality of objectivity in their poems. Whereas Keats and Hazlitt had posited that subjective experience in poetry could be so powerfully empathic as to blur the limits of identity, many of the leading Modernist doctrines—Hulme's classical revival, Yeats' mask and anti-self, Eliot's objective correlative—represented attempts to escape altogether from the limitations of personality, and thus to

present the illusion of experience apprehended directly, not
through the medium of a lyric speaker's sensibility. If knowl-
edge could not be certain, at least it could be real. Karsten
Harries traces from Kant's *Critique of Judgment* the peculiarly
modern notion of the self-sufficiency of the aesthetic expe-
rience. The modern artist sacrifices the idea of universal truth,
and "in its place he offers us a self-sufficient presence, strong
enough to lead us to accept it instead of referring us to some-
thing beyond the poem."[10] This shift in epistemological stance
was accompanied by a changing position toward the reader.
Since subjectivity was suspect, the poet could no longer speak
with authority from the distance imposed by superior vision.
A method had to be devised to draw the reader more im-
mediately into the experience of the poem.

The Imagist movement, the most important single devel-
opment in modern British and American poetry, emerged as
a direct response to these historical and philosophical changes.
Pound conceived Imagism as a corrective to what he saw as
the excesses of late Romanticism: "emotional slither," stale
abstractions, flaccid, merely decorative language. Imagism in-
tended to "make it new" through precise, "explicit rendering"
of experience. Immediacy of feeling and sensation would be
achieved through presentational rather than interpretive struc-
tures:

> The apparition of these faces in the crowd;
> Petals on a wet, black bough.

The reader of the Imagist poem thus occupies a different po-
sition from that of the Romantic descriptive lyric: no longer
simply observers of the visionary moment, we must some-
how learn to share it—by making the associative leap between
the two lines of Pound's couplet—in order to understand its
meaning. The poem's surface is discontinuous; we learn to
read it by intuiting the underlying continuity. At the same
time, the poem's meaning is fully determined by the poet, as
the semicolon (a colon in some printings) suggests and Pound's
account of the genesis of the poem confirms. The reader re-

creates rather than invents the vision, though it is our *illusion* of inventing it—or at least of arriving at it independently—that gives the poem its power and charm.

The Imagist movement itself was short-lived, largely because of the inherent limitations of the form, but its influence has been crucial. Modernism is frequently defined in terms of presentational rather than discursive strategies, of direct and "impersonal" modes of meaning. The disjunctive surface of *The Waste Land* causes the reader to participate in a process of active discovery; its spatial and temporal dislocations and collage of voices force us to supply missing connections, as if we were confronting experience unmediated by any subjective perspective. Yet repeated acquaintance with the poem reveals how fully it is, in fact, governed by an essentially Symbolist poetic. Eliot's complex symbolic design (drought, water, fire), his mythic scaffolding of Fisher King and Grail Quest, even the overriding title—all point to coherent and fully determined meanings beyond the fragmented surface. Several critics have noted the paradox that Eliot's "anonymous style" is so informed by enormous erudition and powerful intentionality—as revealed in modes of satire, parody, and castigation—as to present very fully the image of the "implied author," not anonymous at all. As we have learned more about the biographical circumstances under which the poem was written, it has come more and more to seem at least in part a covert spiritual and psychic autobiography. Even the note naming Tiresias as protagonist, however belatedly added, serves to unite the poem as the experience of a single self; as Robert Langbaum says, "since the protagonist plays at one and the same time both active and passive roles, we must understand all the characters as aspects or projections of his consciousness—that the poem is essentially a monodrama. It is difficult to say just where the various characters melt into the protagonist and where the protagonist melts into the poet."[11] Eliot's peculiar aversion to Romanticism turns out to mask a strongly Romantic temperament.

Equally strong, I would maintain, is the sense of the "implied reader."[12] I read *The Waste Land* primarily as a poem about the fate of culture, and as such it depends crucially on the reader's recognition of its astonishing treatment of cultural fragments and conventions. Someone who did not share this recognition—one not highly educated in the Western tradition, for example—might well be able to read and respond to the poem, but the intention that I believe the poem projects would not be fully achieved. In this sense, though the reader of *The Waste Land* is more directly involved in the discovery of meaning than the reader of "Tintern Abbey," or even of "In a Station of the Metro," that meaning is primarily located in the predetermined symbolic structure of the text and not in the activity of reading. As Marjorie Perloff says, "however difficult it may be to decode this complex poem, the relationship of the word to its referents, of signifier to signified, remains essentially intact."[13] This seems to me equally true of other prototypical Modernist texts, from *The Tower* and *Ulysses* to *The Bridge* and *The Sound and the Fury*. Their tendency toward organic unity and coherence, toward the integration of parts into a coherent symbolic whole determined by the author, marks the degree to which they are still rooted in the symbolist (and Romantic) tradition.

It is in this context that the work of Wallace Stevens and William Carlos Williams is most strikingly original. In many respects they resemble the other High Modernists. They are both the direct descendents of the Romantics in their persistent concern with the relation between the perceiving consciousness and the perceived world of objects. The work of each demonstrates a deeply Romantic temperament: Williams' in its emphasis on the creative dialectic between forces of creation and destruction, Stevens' in its extension of the dilemma of Romantic dualism to meditations on the problem of belief. Both crucially affirm the transcendental value of imagination, yet in both—as in the other modern masters—this is countered: in Stevens by powerful skepticism and recognition of the indifference of the universe to human endeavor, and in Williams by the anti-transcendental urge to root down, to establish immediate contact with the banal and the common-place.

Stevens and Williams both were influenced early by Im-agism, and though they soon abandoned the form because it seemed to them static and unsuitable for embodying the ac-tive, fluctuating world each wanted to project, they remained true to its principles of clear, vital images and fidelity to ex-perience. Each adopted strategies of objectification and anti-sentimentalism. Their poems, like Eliot's and Pound's, rep-resent a concerted response to the twin problems of alienation from nature and a suspect subjectivity. But despite all these links to the tradition, many of the poems of Stevens and Williams may be said to differ, in their rhetorical strategy and the relationship they establish with their reader, from the characteristic Romantic and High Modernist forms—to differ so strongly as to anticipate tendencies we now call postmod-ernist. The particular form these two poets evolved inde-pendently marks a development in modern poetry the im-portance of which has not been generally recognized.

For example, Ralph W. Rader begins a recent article by saying, "The most distinctive and highly valued poems of the modern era offer an image of a dramatized 'I' acting in a concrete setting." He goes on to divide these poems into two genres, dramatic lyric and dramatic monologue, which he differentiates according to the relationship the poem estab-lishes with the reader's own experience: "The sense we have that the experience in [the dramatic lyric] is cognate with our own experience of the natural world is distinctly different from the somewhat parallel sense we have in the dramatic monologue. There we are pleased to feel that the world of the poem is exactly *like* the real world; in the dramatic lyric we have a clear sense that the experience in effect takes place *in* the real world, the world we and the poet are in."[14] Rader's useful distinction allows us to see that in both these lyric forms the reader ultimately confronts the experience of the poem as an outsider; although the world of both dramatic lyric and dramatic monologue is "cognate with" our own, we are dis-

tanced from the experience of that world by our recognition
of the independent, dramatized lyric speaker.

One wonders what Rader's reaction would be to Stevens'
"The Snow Man" (CP, 9-10):

> One must have a mind of winter
> To regard the frost and the boughs
> Of the pine-trees crusted with snow;
>
> And have been cold a long time
> To behold the junipers shagged with ice,
> The spruces rough in the distant glitter
>
> Of the January sun; and not to think
> Of any misery in the sound of the wind,
> In the sound of a few leaves,
>
> Which is the sound of the land
> Full of the same wind
> That is blowing in the same bare place
>
> For the listener, who listens in the snow,
> And, nothing himself, beholds
> Nothing that is not there and the nothing that is.

The surface of this poem is coherent, even seamless, as op-
posed to the disjunctions of the two poems I examined in my
preface. Yet attention to "The Snow Man" reveals the degree
to which its rhetorical stance undermines the expected dis-
cursive conventions. Clearly, there is no dramatized "I" here;
the voice of the poem is disembodied, its impulse not inher-
ently dramatic but descriptive, even didactic. Its purpose is
simply to define the kind of vision necessary in Crispin's
"starker, barer world," to suggest that in a time of disbelief
and spiritual poverty one must adopt an attitude of radical
scepticism, stripped of preconceptions. The answer to the
problem of alienation, the poem maintains, is to merge the
noumenal in the phenomenal world, to regard the wintry
landscape with a mind equally cold and clear.

Yet despite the descriptive intent of the poem, the experience of reading it is necessarily dramatic, as the title emphasizes. There is no snow man in "The Snow Man"—at least, none the reader can observe objectively. The voice of the poem is certainly not the snow man's, nor does it describe the experience of seeing one; rather, it requires the reader to *enter* the snow man, to become "nothing himself" and look out at a blank world through crystalline eyes. Just as the snow man is merged with the landscape by virtue of the fact that he is literally composed of the same substance that blankets the fields, the reader can understand the poem only by imaginatively entering the process it describes. The meaning of the poem is not in an achieved, localized experience described to the reader—as in "Tintern Abbey"—but in the experience of vision the reader undergoes. The poem itself is thus not the record of an action, but its efficient cause.

In a sense, of course, every poem demands the reader's imaginative participation, and thus establishes a dialectic in the act of reading. The distinction I am trying to draw will be apparent in comparing "The Snow Man" to "Stopping by Woods on a Snowy Evening," a poem Rader uses as an example of dramatic lyric. Frost's poem is a model of subtlety and restraint; its beauty lies in the tension its hypnotically understated language can be seen to reveal. Its landscape is "cognate with" the real world, and serves both to localize the speaker's experience and to establish his mood. The act of reading the poem consists largely of discovering what strong currents surge under the placid surface—in other words, of making explicit what is already implicit in the poem. "The Snow Man," on the other hand, remains hypothetical until the reader enacts it, as its extended periodic construction suggests. Its sustained movement from hypothesis ("One must have a mind of winter / . . . not to think / Of any misery in the sound of the wind") to description ("the same wind / That is blowing in the same bare place") *requires* our imaginative participation; there is no speaker as central presence in the landscape of the poem, without the reader. The wintry scene remains naturalistic and not symbolically present in the poem itself; rather, the poem becomes a vehicle for finding coherence in the world beyond it. While the chief dialectic in "Stopping by Woods" is between the speaker and nature, the central dialectic in "The Snow Man" is between the reader and the poem. Thus the act of reading becomes analogous to the sympathetic imaginative union with the phenomenal world that the Romantics persistently sought; the poem itself becomes, in Williams' phrase, "a field of action" (SE, 280).

"The Snow Man," in short, represents a lyric form demonstrably different from the dramatic lyric and the dramatic monologue—a form I propose to call the transparent lyric. Replacing the poet (or the lyric speaker, a poet-surrogate) with the reader as the center of dramatic attention, the poem becomes a transparent medium, a *process* of poetic activity rather than its product. The form itself thus has epistemological significance; as the subjective lens implicit in the dramatic lyric is shifted aside, the reader seems to confront the experience captured in the poem spontaneously and directly. The transparent lyric may be defined as a poem whose rhetoric establishes its own incompleteness; it is presented not as completed discourse but as a structure that invites the reader to project himself or herself into its world, and thus to verify it as contiguous with reality. In imitating the process of thinking, of confronting the world and responding to it, the poem engages the reader in a different way from poetry grounded in an expressive theory of art, and thus requires a different kind of criticism.

To try to account for the simultaneous development of transparence in the work of Stevens and Williams is, of course, a nearly impossible task, given the mysteries of the creative process and the wide variety of influences operating on both poets. One might mention, for instance, the early enthusiasm each felt for Whitman's democratic energies and expansiveness, or for the new philosophers like Whitehead and Santayana; or the general conviction, intensified by the Imagist movement, that nineteenth-century poetic idioms were outdated and in need of daring renovation. But surely one important clue is the fact that Stevens and Williams were the two poets of their generation most influenced by the new art movements determined to break the mold of fixed perspective, and to make art actual and immediate by eliciting the viewer's vital imagination. It is convenient to date this influence from the Armory Show of 1913, where such artists as Cézanne, Gauguin, Renoir, Picasso, Picabia, Duchamp, and Gleizes were seen publicly in New York for the first time.[15] The letters and essays of both Stevens and Williams testify to the enormous excitement each felt at discovering the work of these painters, and to their continuing involvement with modern painting throughout their lives.[16] It seems of great significance to the development of transparence in their work, then, that as Marjorie Perloff demonstrates, in the modern visual arts the break from Symbolism was particularly apparent:

> In painting and sculpture . . . the stage in which surface is preferred to "depth," *process* to *structure*, is much more readily identifiable than it is in poetry. From the early days of Cubism in 1910 through Vorticism and Futurism, Dada and Surrealism, down to the Abstract Expressionism of the fifties, and the Conceptual Art, Super-Realism, assemblages, and performance art of the present, visual artists have consistently resisted the Symbolist model in favor of the creation of a world in which forms can exist "littéralement et dans tous les sens," an oscillation between representational reference and compositional game.[17]

This oscillation is strikingly similar to what I will be calling the double vision of the transparent lyric.

Stevens and Williams had different favorites among the modern painters, of course. Stevens admired the brilliant light and color of the Impressionists and the clarity and structural inventiveness of the Cubists, while important influences on Williams would also include the photography of Alfred Stieglitz and the work of the American Precisionist painters influ-

enced by him, as well as the experiments of Dada and sur-
realism: Cézanne, Matisse, and Braque on the one hand; Juan
Gris, Charles Demuth, and Duchamp on the other. But de-
spite the variety of schools and styles that have been adduced
as influences, a number of common tendencies may be seen
to link them. One is the urge to escape glib illusionism through
a self-conscious emphasis on the materials of the artwork
itself, its canvas and paint and brush strokes. By frankly ac-
knowledging its own status as a fiction, a deliberate construc-
tion, the work of art could attain a liberating vitality and
immediacy. Williams and Stevens were among the first (along
with Gertrude Stein) to recognize the literary applications of
this principle. As Williams said, it is the attempt "to come
over into the tactile qualities, the words themselves beyond
the mere thought expressed that distinguishes the modern, or
distinguished the modern of that time from the period before
the turn of the century" (A, 380).

A related concern of most of these movements—particu-
larly Cubism and Precisionism—was the attempt to balance
a radically personal vision with the scrupulous measure of
aesthetic form. For example:

> Precisionism's most famous principle held that each pic-
> ture, regardless of its "objective" content, was primarily
> a portrait of emotion itself—an objective correlative.
> . . . In seeking to find Equivalents for emotion, how-
> ever, the Precisionists felt that the artist's own presence
> must be impersonal, even invisible. This . . . premise—
> that the ideal artist is as selfless as a lens—means that
> the emotions that are expressed in Precisionist art are
> not located in a particular place, time, or personality.[18]

This directly parallels Michel Benamou's claim about the re-
lation of Stevens' aesthetic to Impressionism: "In a sense, his
aesthetics were Cézanne's subjective ('expressing oneself') ob-
jectivism ('realizing the object'). It is a personal meeting, an
encounter with reality on terms of equality."[19] James Breslin
has noted the effect of the automatic writing of the surrealists

on Williams' improvisational prose, *Kora in Hell* (1920): "We are required to yield whatever fixed point of view we bring to the work; we must surrender *our* conscious personality and let ourselves be drawn in. To put it another way, the reader is forced to experience the work from the inside; aesthetic distance is disintegrated."[20] The transparent lyric compounds this process, by allowing the reader to experience the work from inside and outside at once: we seem to enter the world of the poem directly and immediately, at the same time being continually reminded that this world is the poet's fictional composition. As Williams says, "If I succeed in keeping myself objective enough, sensual enough, I can produce the factors, the concretions of materials by which others shall understand and so be led to use—that they may better see, touch, taste, enjoy—their own world *differing as it may* from mine" (SE, 197-98).

In the aesthetic of modern painting Williams and Stevens discovered a new relation between art and its audience that each found genuinely liberating. Williams was enthusiastic about Apollinaire's *Les Peintres cubistes* (1913), which includes this claim: "Representing planes to denote volumes, Picasso gives so complete and so decisive an enumeration of the various elements which make up the object that these do not take the shape of the object. This is largely due to the effort of the viewer, who is forced to see all the elements simultaneously just because of the way they have been arranged."[21] Similarly, "to Stevens . . . transparence brought participation. His comments on the Impressionists bespoke his delight that their art removed a barrier between him and nature."[22] It is not surprising, then, that two poets so deeply affected by such an aesthetic in painting might begin to experiment with ways to allow their readers to experience more directly the "nature" of their poems—whether that nature constituted a young sycamore, the metaphysics suggested by a glass of water, or the urgent presence of a red wheelbarrow. "Just as the painter transforms reality into a reality on canvas, that new reality prepares the observer, in the constant interplay between art

and nature, to return to the actual, and discover there what
he had not realized before."[23] In the transparent lyric Stevens
and Williams found a means to bring vitality and immediacy
to the art-object by rendering meaning in terms of the process
of reading.

The transparent lyric as I have described it resembles the
internalized form defined by Louis Martz as the poetry of
meditation, but there are important differences between the
two. The form of the meditative poem, which Martz traces
from seventeenth-century religious exercises and extends spe-
cifically to the work of Stevens and Williams, reflects the
drama of a projected self applying to some crucial problem
"the willed and reasoned structures of the mind."[24] The trans-
parent lyric, as exemplified by Stevens and Williams, is a more
open, inclusive, and—I would argue—specifically "modern"
form; although it frequently employs the movement of con-
certed meditation, often it reflects such other acts of the mind
as the kind of double-edged perception demonstrated by Wil-
liams' "The Snow Begins" (PB, 56):

> A rain of bombs, well placed,
> is no less lovely
> but this comes gently over all
>
> all crevices are covered
> the stalks of
> fallen flowers vanish before
>
> this benefice all the garden's
> wounds are healed
> white, white, white as death
>
> fallen which dignifies it as
> no violence ever can
> gently and silently in the night.

Here the field of consciousness shifts between the images of
snow and bombs so subtly as to achieve ironies far beyond
the reach of simple metaphor, and perceptions that cannot be

characterized as "willed and reasoned structures." The pur-
pose of meditative poetry is fairly consistently to enable "the
human being to compose a sensitive, intelligent, and generous
self," Martz tells us, and he describes Stevensian meditation
as "attentive thinking about concrete things with the aim of
developing an affectionate understanding of how good it is
to be alive."[25] As illuminating as Martz's approach in general
is, to suggest that Stevens' and Williams' style may be ade-
quately defined in terms of this tradition is finally to risk
distortion. The profound disorder and constant flux of the
natural world are of crucial importance for both poets; poetry
which is to resist successfully the pressure of reality without
evading it must somehow reflect that flux. Thus, while Ste-
vens' and Williams' poems are acts of self-creation, they also
embody the ironic process of decreation or demythification.
By focusing dramatically on the process of vision, they force
us to recognize that imaginative coherence is local and sub-
jective. And the transparent lyric, invariably self-conscious,
is an appropriate medium for this complicated action; while
often moving toward moments of harmony between man and
nature, such poems remind us simultaneously that the "self"
and "world" of which that harmony is composed are fictive
and transitory. Deeply mimetic of the shifting, ephemeral
nature of all experience, they never allow us to rest secure in
any fixed, comfortable pattern of seeing or thinking.

Order, in other words, always remains an *idea* of order.
Stevens' poem of that title is well-known, but it is also fre-
quently misunderstood. "The Idea of Order at Key West"
(CP, 128-30) is a variant of the transparent lyric, though it
embodies the dramatized "I" normally characteristic of the
dramatic lyric. The difference is in locating the center of the
dramatized experience the poem expresses: whereas in the
dramatic lyric the typical pattern of crisis and resolution is
localized in the speaker himself, the speaker of "The Idea of
Order" witnesses a confrontation *outside* himself, which he
internalizes and then expresses. The form of Stevens' poem
might be called an inverted Romantic lyric, a "Tintern Ab-

bey" from Dorothy Wordsworth's perspective, except that
in this case the observer is decidedly not passive, and in fact
plays the central part. The speaker's role in "The Idea of
Order" is analogous to that of the reader of a transparent
lyric; self-consciously distanced from the scene he observes,
he nevertheless invests it imaginatively with a meaning it does
not otherwise have. The poem is thus not the "imperious
allegory"[26] of the creative will so many critics would have it,
but a parable of the delicate relationship between the percep-
tion and the creation of order.

"The Idea of Order" is set in a decidedly non-Wordsworth-
ian landscape. The sea is alien and wholly lacking in imman-
ence; incapable of filling the spiritual role it once held, "like
a body wholly body, fluttering / Its empty sleeves," it grinds
and gasps its wordless song throughout the poem. This na-
turalistic background is crucial; whatever else happens, "the
meaningless plungings of water and the wind" remain unde-
niably present. Nor is the woman who walks on the beach
singing intended simply to represent "the muse of the human
imagination":[27] "The sea was not a mask. No more was she."
She is primarily a woman, a human figure, engaged not in
metaphysics but in song. Thus "the ever-hooded, tragic-ges-
tured sea" of mythical history becomes "merely a place by
which she walked to sing." She is separated from the natural
scene; because she and the ocean speak different languages,
their simultaneous songs cannot merge into unified music:

> The song and water were not medleyed sound
> Even if what she sang was what she heard
> Since what she sang was uttered word by word.
> It may be that in all her phrases stirred
> The grinding water and the gasping wind;
> But it was she and not the sea we heard.

By all rights, the picture must remain divided.

Yet somehow the chaos of two songs is resolved into the
unity of one:

. . . And when she sang, the sea,
Whatever self it had, became the self
That was her song, for she was the maker.

The crux of the poem is in determining the source of that unity. "Whose spirit is this?" we ask. Many critics assume it is the woman's. Denis Donoghue says that she "imposes upon reality her own imagination, until reality is taken up into her song and there is nothing but the song."[28] Frank Doggett's view is parallel: "the music of the singer . . . is the music or order imposed by the will of individual consciousness."[29] But such a poetic statement would be, as Donoghue claims it is, quite unbalanced, since nature obviously has an autonomous existence that is not ruled by imperious will. In claiming that "the figure is all imagination, and the reality—such as it is— is merely a function of the imagination,"[30] Donoghue mistakes the speaker's perception of the event for an expression of the poet's will. The singer is primarily important not as subject but as object of the speaker's creative observation. In fact, Stevens makes it quite clear that the singer's will is not central to the idea of order, and that the landscape remains profoundly disordered (italics added):

. . . it was more than that,
More even than her voice, and ours, among
The meaningless plungings of water and the wind.

But though her song does not change the natural scene, her presence does change the speaker's perception of it, by infusing into what would otherwise be an alien landscape the sense of human value and poignance: "It was her voice that made / The sky acutest at its vanishing. / She measured to the hour its solitude." It is in this sense only—in the momentary conjunction of scene, woman, and speaker—that order may be said to triumph over disorder (italics added):

. . . . Then we,
As we beheld her striding there alone,
Knew that there never was a world for her
Except the one she sang and, singing, made.

"Knowledge" here is not metaphysical but visionary. The
speaker's affirmation is admittedly fictive, since he realizes
that in fact "the water never formed to mind or voice."
But Merle E. Brown's claim that "the title of the poem . . .
should be read in such a way as to suggest that the very idea
of order at Key West is absurd"[31] is unpersuasive. If tran-
scendent order is not possible, the *idea* of order assuredly is,
and the final two stanzas offer compelling proof. The singing
stops, the speaker and his companion turn back toward the
town—and in what he *knows* to be fortuitous phenomena he
sees another vision of order:

> The lights in the fishing boats at anchor there,
> As the night descended, tilting in the air,
> Mastered the night and portioned out the sea,
> Fixing emblazoned zones and fiery poles,
> Arranging, deepening, enchanting night.

Again, the human presence, as represented by the fishing
boats, deepens and enchants the landscape when observed by
an intelligence capable of seeing patterns in chance constel-
lation. Donoghue remarks, "The poet's will demands that
what he thinks be true,"[32] but actually he knows it to be both
true and false—and in that paradox lies all the richness of
Stevens' art. "The final belief is to believe in a fiction, which
you know to be a fiction, there being nothing else" (OP, 163).
Indeed, the final stanza suggests that as the stars which are
our evidence of order grow more dim, the achievements of
the "blessed rage for order" become more valuable. And this
reliance on our own perception of momentary conjunction,
rather than on notions of exterior and stable order, is reflected
in the experience of reading the poem.

I have said that reading a transparent lyric is analogous to
confronting the phenomenal world directly, without benefit
of the overt mediation exercised by a lyric speaker. "The Idea
of Order" both describes and embodies that experience. The
poem begins as a narrative statement, but soon evolves into
a series of questions, both explicit ("Whose spirit is this?"

"tell me, if you know . . .") and implicit (why does the sea "become the self / That was her song"?), to which the reader must supply answers in order to understand the experience. Forced to discover the source of order the speaker perceives, the reader seems to share the experience of the speaker, listening with him to the separate songs of sea and woman and resolving them through his or her own rage for order into momentary coherence. The poem's rhetoric forces the reader to assume an active dramatic role: the ghostlier demarcations of the transparent lyric evoke immediacy, spontaneity, keener sounds.

★

. . . There is a war between the mind
And sky, between thought and day and night. It is
For that the poet is always in the sun,

Patches the moon together in his room
To his Virgilian cadences, up down,
Up down. . . .

(CP, 407)

"It is a war that never ends," precisely because for Stevens the attempt to patch the moon together must begin anew every night. The gap between the self and the world may be bridged by moments of imaginative vision, but "ecstatic identities / Between one's self and the weather" (CP, 258) inevitably fade. Day is always followed by night, credences of summer by the necessary scepticism of a mind of winter. "The law of chaos is the law of ideas, / Of improvisations and seasons of belief" (CP, 255). The extent to which the experience of reading a transparent lyric reflects Stevens' improvisational epistemology may be most clearly seen by reading several examples of the form.

A poem that resists translation into abstract ideas is "What We See Is What We Think" (CP, 459-60). Richard Allen Blessing's analysis is fairly typical:

Critics agree pretty much with Robert Pack that the
poem is a record of the manner in which "seen things
[change] to things thought," or, as Riddel puts it, "Ex-
perience changes to thought and memory." The title
indicates a condition in which experience, seeing, and
what we think, thought and memory, are one and the
same—a condition which exists only at noon. . . . The
pattern of changing images suggests the progression of
any experience as it moves from sensation to thought,
memory, and meditation. Finally, the moment of sen-
sory experience, the vivid green of the morning trees,
degenerates into one of the forms in which we fix and
falsify our being.[33]

Blessing's criticism is generally successful in evoking the dy-
namics of poems, yet here he does not accurately reflect the
reading experience. Calling the poem "reasonably straight-
forward," he implies that the transformation from seeing to
thinking it embodies is direct and unambiguous. But turning
to the poem, we find its language complex and mercurial:

At twelve, the disintegration of afternoon
Began, the return to phantomerei, if not
To phantoms. Till then, it had been the other way:

One imagined the violet trees but the trees stood
    green,
At twelve, as green as ever they would be.
The sky was blue beyond the vaultiest phrase.

Twelve meant as much as: the end of normal time,
Straight up, an élan without harrowing,
The imprescriptible zenith, free of harangue,

Twelve and the first gray second after, a kind
Of violet gray, a green violet, a thread
To weave a shadow's leg or sleeve, a scrawl

On the pedestal, an ambitious page dog-eared
At the upper right, a pyramid with one side
Like a spectral cut in its perception, a tilt

> And its tawny caricature and tawny life,
> Another thought, the paramount ado . . .
> Since what we think is never what we see.

The structure of the poem is in itself complicated: rather than proceeding chronologically, it begins at noon, glances into afternoon, and then returns to morning and the world as it existed until twelve. The morning world, with its sharply defined blues and greens, resists imaginative transfiguration and the embellishments of language ("beyond the vaultiest phrase"). But at noon, as shadows begin to appear, those neat definitions blur; simultaneously, the language takes on playfully protean qualities. The emphasis is not on the perfect balance of noon that Blessing suggests, but on the two opposing states which noon separates. Moreover, we can actually see that shift in the language: noon is that point that divides the rather prosaic "the end of normal time, / Straight up" from the more mysterious phrasing of "an élan without harrowing, / The imprescriptible zenith, free of harangue." We are not told that the lengthening shadows of afternoon correspond to the shades of imagination; rather, we experience them as the voice shifts the terms of the description: "the first gray second after, a kind / Of violet gray, a green violet." The reader, in short, is involved in an experience in which clear, straightforward language ("One imagined the violet trees but the trees stood green") gradually disintegrates into a much shadier, shifting verbal field, evoking not "a record" of a process but the process itself.

The disintegration continues through the rest of the poem. The last four stanzas compose a single sentence whose syntax falls completely apart; what begins as a fairly clear definition of noon turns into a list of objects whose coherence is entirely unspecified. Blessing says confidently, "All of these forms are flawed in some way, are either dog-eared or tawny, are merely caricatures of experience."[34] Yet simply to call the forms degenerate, false, and flawed ignores the wonderful exuberance with which they are summoned. The images are suggestive of a shadow on a sundial, but their peculiar variety prevents us from seeing them simply as a metaphorical "code" for a real object. It is crucial that the process of disintegration is accompanied by an increasingly creative vitality; "the first gray second" that threatens morning's clarity is also "a thread / To weave a shadow's leg or sleeve." The warm, slanting afternoon light is both mocking ("a tawny caricature") and celebratory ("tawny life"). "Phantomerei" implies a liveliness that the static green and blue landscape lacks, while the dog-eared ambitious page may simply be well read. The poem's meaning is bound up in the restless imagination that takes over, and in the way that the images it creates demand the reader's attention and participation.

Like "The Idea of Order," "What We See" begins as narrative description, but before our eyes the world of nature is transformed into a field of extravagant language: the process that is the poem's subject is enacted in the reading experience. Understanding the poem is not simply a matter of following what it says, but of seeing the world in terms of what the poem does. Its movement is increasingly lively, pressing toward the surreal until it breaks into pure idea: "Another thought, the paramount ado. . . ." The final line is thus not a simple reversal of the title; with the experience of the poem behind us, we understand that the exuberant life of the mind could never be contained by any fixed visual scene, that any set of images can be disintegrated and reassembled into countless other forms by the paramount faculty of imagination. The poem is an exercise in the kind of imaginative vision Stevens thought necessary for an adequate comprehension of the world. As he wrote in 1942, "The subject-matter of poetry is not that 'collection of solid, static objects extended in space' but the life that is lived in the scene that it composes; and so reality is not that external scene but the life that is lived in it. Reality is things as they are" (NA, 25). Similarly, the vision of the poem is not external to the reader, but one which the poem's form requires us to enter and share.

"The Glass of Water" (CP, 197-98) is another poem that treats the relationship between the mind and the object in the

form of an exercise in vision. Again, the meaning of the poem
is not primarily in any abstract statement derived from it, but
in the reading experience itself. Stevens begins the poem, as
Joseph Riddel says, wearing his mask of pedagogue:[35]

> That the glass would melt in heat,
> That the water would freeze in cold,
> Shows that this object is merely a state,
> One of many, between two poles. So,
> In the metaphysical, there are these poles.

The glass of water serves as an illustration of the relativity of
matter on the thermodynamic scale. It may also be used, the
disembodied voice continues, to demonstrate metaphysical
poles comparable to the thermal poles of heat and cold. We
are led to expect an elaboration of these poles—being and
nonbeing, perhaps.

But in the demonstration the sharp polarities, like the neat
definitions in "What We See," break down:

> Here in the centre stands the glass. Light
> Is the lion that comes down to drink. There
> And in that state, the glass is a pool.
> Ruddy are his eyes and ruddy are his claws
> When light comes down to wet his frothy jaws
>
> And in the water winding weeds move round.

The fiction of pedagogue slips aside, and although what fol-
lows projects an attitude, it is not developed with enough
dramatic coherence to represent a lyric speaker: what matters
is the play of ideas itself, not their dramatic source. Peda-
gogical lucidity gives way to imaginative exuberance, and the
metaphor is developed in quite another direction and far more
vividly than would be required by the philosophical discussion
with which the poem began. Indeed, we may well ask whether
the image functions as the example of metaphysical polarity
it pretends to be. Most critics apparently believe it does. Rid-
del says, "In the image of light partaking of (thus isolating

and illuming) one of the many possible forms of being, we have a figure of the imagination's several possiblilities,"[36] and Alan Perlis is even more specific: "The lion . . . stands for the potentially violent imagination, temporarily in a state of calm. The glass, placed in the center of nature, is the human mind caught, for the sake of hypothesis, in a fixed position. First it observes light, next the lion."[37]

This kind of criticism seems to me inappropriate to the poem; the image as Perlis describes it is not "merely a state," but a fixed, decodable symbol. I would say just the opposite, that the significance of the metaphor is not seen directly, in any symbolic meaning, but indirectly, in the act of seeing metaphorically, in perceiving the glass touched by a ray of light as a pool where a lion drinks, a process in which we participate in the act of reading. The metaphysical poles, in short, are two ways of seeing: the glass as physical object and the glass as African landscape. And the spectrum between them—in another poem Stevens calls it "the flux / Between the thing as idea and / The idea as thing" (CP, 295)—is defined by the reader's mind in the act of reading the poem. We have been asked to move a great distance from the beginning of the poem, and are required to move farther still. The glass of water as pedagogical tool is left behind, and the clear, polarized distinctions jumble and blur:

> And there and in another state—the refractions,
> The *metaphysica*, the plastic parts of poems
> Crash in the mind—But, fat Jocundus, worrying
> About what stands here in the centre, not the glass,
>
> But in the centre of our lives, this time, this day,
> It is a state, this spring among the politicians
> Playing cards. In a village of the indigenes,
> One would have still to discover. Among the dogs
> and dung,
> One would continue to contend with one's ideas.

Fat Jocundus, as Blessing says, is clearly not the poet, since "the poet is precisely the man who most realizes that there is

no center, but that there are only 'states,' and that life is a
process of continuous discovery."[38] Nevertheless, he deserves
a civil answer to his question about what stands at the center;
the new refraction, the village of the indigenes, is both no
answer and the best answer. It is an arbitrary "state," but no
less arbitrary than the apparently stable glass of water. Jo-
cundus must learn that any image may stand at the center of
our lives—or, rather, that the kind of vision that invents "the
plastic parts of poems" may. In the world washed by the
imagination, we can all be indigenes.

Stevens' late and rarely discussed "Note on Moonlight"
(CP, 531-32) is one of his most subtle and moving explora-
tions of the role of vision in uniting self and world. It appears
almost too straightforward to need analysis, yet understand-
ing it requires the reader to make delicate shifts of attention
and perception. The poem plays the traditional association of
moonlight with imaginative transformation against a natu-
ralistic view of moonlight as clear illumination—in other words,
it juxtaposes the two epistemological poles suggested in "The
Glass of Water." The opening simile compares moonlight to
the process of thought, while stressing the objectiveness of
the objects of attention:

> The one moonlight, in the simple-colored night,
> Like a plain poet revolving in his mind
> The sameness of his various universe,
> Shines on the mere objectiveness of things.

The poet is clearly Stevens in the act of writing this poem,
but as we read his language and follow where the poem leads,
the peculiarly abstracted nature of the experience ("the one
moonlight," "shines on the mere objectiveness") and the ab-
sence of dramatic definition serve to draw us more immedi-
ately into the process. This movement is paradigmatic of the
transparent lyric; the poem defines a central role which does
not simply represent the poet, and which the reader must
inhabit in order to understand the imaginative action of the
poem.

In the moonlight, the landscape gains order and coherence:

"It is as if being was to be observed." Conversely, the presence
of objects gives purpose to the moonlight; the essential "prop-
erty of the moon" seems to be "what it evokes." The alchemy
of moonlight—and, following the simile, of meditation—works
in either of two ways:

> It is to disclose the essential presence, say,
> Of a mountain, expanded and elevated almost
> Into a sense, an object the less; or else
>
> To disclose in the figure waiting on the road
> An object the more, an undetermined form
> Between the slouchings of a gunman and a lover,
> A gesture in the dark, a fear one feels
>
> In the great vistas of night air, that takes this form,
> In the arbors that are as if of Saturn-star.

The clear, undifferentiated light in fact affects different objects
differently, elevating some into ghostly forms and revealing
others as menacingly real. And this polarity is reflected in the
experience of the poem; the image of the mountain and its
relation to whoever perceives it remain vague and unsub-
stantial, while the "slouchings of a gunman and a lover" are
vital and evocative. Obviously, the light that seems uniformly
objective is in fact not, and acts to vary the sameness of the
natural world:

> So, then, this warm, wide, weatherless quietude
> Is active with a power, an inherent life,
>
> In spite of the mere objectiveness of things,
> Like a cloud-cap in the corner of a looking-glass,
> A change of color in the plain poet's mind,
> Night and silence disturbed by an interior sound.
>
> The one moonlight, the various universe, intended
> So much just to be seen—a purpose, empty
> Perhaps, absurd perhaps, but at least a purpose,
> Certain and ever more fresh. Ah! Certain, for sure . . .

The allusion to *The Tempest* ("The baseless fabric of this vi-
sion, / The cloud-capp'd towers, the gorgeous palaces . . .")
is richly appropriate, since the modest claims made here for
moonlight are parallel to Prospero's rough magic, which de-
pends entirely on the power of illusion and fictive vision for
its effect. Given the delicate modulation, Stevens' affirmation
of the purpose of imagination is entirely without irony. In
the final stanzas, Stevens' style achieves its distinctive power
by shifting carefully between the dramatic and the transparent.
On the one hand, the rhetoric is discursive ("So, then . . . ,"
"Ah! Certain, for sure"); on the other hand, the poem pro-
ceeds not by discursive logic but by association and juxta-
position (which establish, for example, a persuasive relation
between moonlight and "a change of color in the plain poet's
mind"). The reader experiences not an idea projected by a
lyric speaker, but the idea itself, seemingly first-hand. To
understand the poem, we must move into the field of asso-
ciative consciousness and participate in the process of trans-
formation. And this movement in turn allows us to approach
what Stevens described as that "degree of participation at
which what is real and what is imagined are one: a state of
clairvoyant observation, accessible or possibly accessible to
the poet, say, the acutest poet" (OP, 166). Through the rhet-
oric of the transparent lyric we share that clairvoyance and
acuteness to an extraordinary degree.

2

The Theater and the Book

The thinker as reader reads what has been written,
He wears the words he reads to look upon
Within his being,

A crown within him of crispest diamonds,
A reddened garment falling to his feet,
A hand of light to turn the page,

A finger with a ring to guide his eye
From line to line, as we lie on the grass and listen
To that which has no speech,

The voluble intentions of the symbols,
The ghostly celebrations of the picnic,
The secretions of insight.

                    Stevens, "Things of August"

"Nowadays it is common-place to speak of the role of the
writer in the world of today. But why not think and speak
of the role of the reader in the world of today: the role of the
reader of *Origines*, the role of the reader of my poetry, say,
in the midst of the contemporary conspiracy and in the midst
of the contemporary conspirators" (L, 599). Stevens' imme-
diate subject in this 1948 letter to José Rodríguez Feo is the
difficulty and apparent futility of reading in the midst of the
overwhelming reality of contemporary history. But his state-
ment invites more general speculation about the role he ex-
pected the reader of his own poems to play. Because this

question is seldom considered in studies of Stevens,[1] our understanding of the nature of his achievement has been limited. We are still far from knowing with assurance how to read many of his poems. Using the rhetoric of the transparent lyric, Stevens carefully constructed a role for his reader; examining that role helps to reveal his work's subtlety and experimental range.

Much recent criticism, in its concern to link Stevens with the Romantic tradition, treats the poems purely as acts of self-expression.[2] The expressivist approach finds its most extreme form in the neo-Freudian "misreadings" of Harold Bloom, as based on the conviction that "the language of British and American poetry, from at least Wordsworth to the present, is overdetermined in its patternings, and so necessarily is underdetermined in its meanings." This assumption allows him to state, for example, that Stevens begins his "Domination of Black" with "what the Freudians, in their tropological system, call a 'reaction formation,' a defensive movement of the spirit that is opposed to a repressed desire, and so manifests itself as a reaction against that desire."[3] But expressive theories of literature, suggesting faithful transcriptions of internal landscapes, spontaneous overflows of powerful feelings, apply only minimally to Stevens, for whom art was always as much a matter of communication as of self-expression, and who always wrote with one eye on his audience. His letters to scholars and translators abound with attempts to clarify the meanings of his poems. As inadequate as he felt the resulting paraphrases often were, he was nevertheless willing to make them, judging that his poems should not be difficult for the reader who approached them from the proper perspective: "I have always thought that to the right reader my poems were perfectly clear" (L, 710). While Stevens never denied the importance of inspiration and genuine feeling in poetry, he dispensed with the mysticism that often accompanies Romantic theories of imagination: "Writing poetry is a conscious activity. While poems may very well occur, they had very much better be caused" (L, 274). For Stevens, poetry was a deliberate, self-conscious art, designed to speak to "the delicatest ear of the mind" (CP, 240) of an actual reader.

In addition to his conviction that poetry was fundamentally an act of communication, Stevens also wrote under the assumption that "to read a poem should be an experience, like experiencing an act" (OP, 164). His letters are explicit about his feeling that the essential aspect of poetry is that which sets it apart from its paraphrasable ideas: in 1952 he wrote to Sister M. Bernetta Quinn, "If I felt the obligation to pursue the philosophy of my poems, I should be writing philosophy, not poetry; and it is poetry that I want to write" (L, 753). To another correspondent, he wrote in 1945 that "the point of ['The Emperor of Ice-Cream'] is not its meaning. When people think of poems as integrations, they are thinking usually of integration of ideas; that is to say, of what they mean. However, a poem must have a peculiarity, as if it was the momentarily complete idiom of that which prompts it, even if that which prompts it is the vaguest emotion" (L, 500). Moreover, he clearly felt that the "peculiarity" beyond ideas was ultimately the chief reason for reading and writing poems. One measure of this belief is the enthusiasm he expresses in his 1937 lecture "The Irrational Element in Poetry" for the arbitrary experiments of surrealist poetry, which often lacked paraphrasable content altogether:

> They are extraordinarily alive and that they make it possible for us to read poetry that seems filled with gaiety and youth, just when we were beginning to despair of gaiety and youth, is immensely to the good. . . . Those who seek for the freshness and strangeness of poetry in fresh and strange places do so because of an intense need.   (OP, 228)

Yet this freshness and strangeness are precisely the elements most often neglected by recent criticism, which is devoted for the most part to an explication of Stevens' ideas. Of course Stevens' work is modeled on a cohesive and carefully elaborated philosophical core, whose importance it would be im-

possible to deny. But explication must be balanced by atten-
tion to the strikingly original texture of the poems. The great
achievement of his art, as of all important literature, is not
simply its ideas but the particular qualities of its language and
form. The poems require, and have not often received, careful
consideration of the immediate experience of actually reading
them.

Increasingly often throughout his career, and particularly
in his late, great meditative poems, Stevens asks his readers
not only to comprehend his various acts of perception, cog-
nition, and association, but to perform them with him. The
act of reading the poem thus becomes analogous to the act of
writing it, and in turn to sharing in the process of imaginative
transformation that for Stevens was the only credible source
of order and value. The idea of relation between the poet's
and the reader's minds is of course a Romantic commonplace;
again, it is the particular way in which the experience of
reading a poem by Stevens extends that idea that is his most
important achievement. "The poet seems to confer his iden-
tity on the reader. It is easiest to recognize this when listening
to music—I mean this sort of thing: the transference" (OP,
158). The analogy to music is significant, suggesting that the
rhythm, the dynamics, the mood are all essential elements of
what is to be transferred. Stevens makes clear that the poet
must convey not only ideas but the process of thought, not
merely the things imagined but the whole imagination, and
that this "vivid transparence" (CP, 380) is a project of the
greatest importance: "I think that his function is to make his
imagination theirs and that he fulfills himself only as he sees
his imagination become the light in the minds of others. His
role, in short, is to help people to live their lives" (NA, 29).
As one of Stevens' aphorisms suggests, the result for the reader
is a peculiar state in which the imagination both is and is not
one's own: "When the mind is like a hall in which thought
is like a voice speaking, the voice is always that of someone
else" (OP, 168). This extraordinary doubleness is a crucial
element of Stevens' work. We may explore it by examining

two images that recur in his poems, those of the theater and
the book, both of which become metaphors for precisely the
relationship between reader and poem that I am attempting
to define.

★

It might seem sheer folly to begin with a discussion of the
dramatic aspect of Stevens' work, since the critics seem to be
in virtually complete agreement that his poetry is not dra-
matic. In 1932, R. P. Blackmur stated quite firmly,

> Mr. Stevens is not a dramatic poet. Instead of drama-
> tizing his feelings, he takes as fatal the drama that he
> sees and puts it down either in its least dramatic, most
> meditative form, or makes of it a simple statement. . . .
> A dramatic poet . . . molds wholes out of parts them-
> selves autonomous. Mr. Stevens, not a dramatic poet,
> seizes his wholes only in imagination; in his poems the
> parts are already connected. . . . To the dramatic style
> his talents were unsuitable, and if by chance he used it,
> it would prevent both the meditative mood and the
> accent of intellectual wit which he needed to make the
> subject his own.[4]

For Randall Jarrell, too, Stevens' interest in solitary, intro-
spective meditation automatically displaces the possibility of
externalized dramatic action: "How little there is in Stevens,
ordinarily, of the narrative, dramatic, immediately active side
of life, of harried actors compelled, impelled, in ignorant hope.
But how much is there of the man who looks, feels, meditates,
in the freedom of removedness, of disinterested imagining,
of thoughtful love!"[5] Similarly, Hugh Kenner has lamented
what he takes to be the general failure of Stevens' poems to
engage their reader dramatically: "There is a great deal of
language in these poems, with no one speaking it except the
grave impersonal voice of poetry, and there is little variety
of feeling. The most that happens is that the voice turns

whimsical. That grave equable voice, as dispassionate as *things*, weaves its whimsical monologue. . . . In Stevens' world, there are no actions and no speeches, merely ways of looking at things."[6]

Early in his career, Stevens was intensely interested in theater. In 1916 and 1917 he wrote three plays, *Three Travelers Watch a Sunrise, Carlos Among the Candles,* and *Bowl, Cat and Broomstick,* all of which were produced in New York. But each altogether failed to provide audiences with dramatic interest, tension, characterization, or distinguished language, sharing instead the interest in fey "effects" and delicate atmosphere that marked much of the experimental American theater of the time. The action of *Carlos,* for example, consists entirely of the single character's appropriately dreamy monologue as he lights and then extinguishes two dozen candles. Stevens recognized his apparent failure "to have the play a play and not merely a poem" (L, 194), and, like Henry James two decades earlier, retired from the stage in considerable discomfort. Samuel French Morse carries this failure over into his evaluation of the poems: "the plays bear out the judgment often made on Stevens, that his poetry is dramatically weak" (OP, xxx).

Yet surely it is possible to suggest different conclusions: that his failures on the stage determined Stevens, again like James, to apply his dramatic interest instead to the genre most congenial to his talent, and that while we should expect his poems to be less overtly theatrical than the naturalistic dialogues of Frost or the ventriloquial collages of Eliot, they may still incorporate dramatic elements in a subtler form. Certainly, Stevens never lost his interest in drama; eighteen years after the failure of his plays he commented, "I think it quite likely that I should have been more interested in the theater if those two experiments had not given me the horrors" (L, 291), and as late as 1949 he appears, rather surprisingly, to have seriously entertained the notion of writing a play for puppets (L, 627). He was also eager to extend the conventional boundaries of theater, once suggesting that "a theatre without

action or characters ought to be within the range of human
interests" (L, 203). A theater without action or characters is
difficult to conceive; in such a theater the stage would remain
bare, and the possibility for dramatic action would rest solely
within the imagination of the audience. Each spectator would
thus be catapulted onto center stage, forced in essence to be-
come the playwright and to invent the play he or she has
come to see. This is of course to suggest an imperfect analogy;
far from being purely conceptual art, Stevens' poems are fully,
arrestingly imagined. At the same time, their intended effect
is not that of a fixed, objective model, but of a scenario for
the theater of acts of the mind. Their meaning requires the
active participation of the reader's imagination, and insofar
as they receive it, they are deeply, if subtly, dramatic. Im-
mediately following his claim that the poems lack drama,
Randall Jarrell continues:

> As we read the poems we are so continually aware of
> Stevens observing, meditating, creating, that we feel like
> saying that the process of creating the poem is the poem.
> Surprisingly often the motion of qualification, of
> concession, of logical conclusion . . . is the movement
> that organizes the poem; and in Stevens the unlikely
> tenderness of this movement—the one, the not-quite-
> that, the other, the not-exactly-the-other, the real one,
> the real other—is like the tenderness of the sculptor or
> draftsman, whose hand makes but looks as if it caressed.[7]

From the relationship between this movement and the reader's
tracing of it, Stevens constructs an intricate drama of sensi-
bility. Or as he more simply says, "Authors are actors, books
are theatres" (OP, 157).

It should be clear that Stevens' characteristic form is not
that of dramatic monologue. As Robert Langbaum persua-
sively defines it in *The Poetry of Experience*, the central action
of the dramatic monologue is psychological, often creating
tension between the reader's sympathy and moral judgment,
and culminating in the ultimate "victory of character over

action."[8] In Stevens' poems the reader's role depends upon the near-transparence of character, and the movement of lyric expression itself becomes a kind of dramatic action. Nevertheless, much of Langbaum's commentary does serve to describe Stevens' work, and to suggest why his direct appeal to the reader's imagination can be viewed as a response to the Romantic problem of epistemological dualism:

> Whether the poetry of experience starts out to be lyrical or dramatic, . . . to the extent that it imitates the structure of experience, to the extent that its meaning is a movement of perception, it must be in final effect much the same—both lyrical and dramatic, subjective and objective: a poetry dealing with the object and the eye on the object.[9]

The Stevens poem is a theater of imagination in which the reader is asked to imitate the roles of both playwright and actor—figures, respectively, of the creative impulse and its fulfillment. Reading the poem, then, we come to embody simultaneously subject and object, to become both "the idea and the bearer-being of the idea" (CP, 466).

Stevens frequently uses the metaphor of the theater to express his idea of the complex, reciprocal relationship between the self and the world. Often in his early poetry the actor, an acquiescent Everyman, learns his role from the stage setting, and thus assimilates himself into his environment. Crispin, in "The Comedian as the Letter C," comes to realize that "the natives of the rain are rainy men" (CP, 37), and numerous personae in *Harmonium* subscribe to the "Theory" that "I am what is around me" (CP, 86). It is, of course, possible to claim to have invented the world, as the speaker in "Tea at the Palaz of Hoon" does—"I was the world in which I walked, and what I saw / Or heard or felt came not but from myself" (CP, 65)—but not without imprisoning oneself in a mirrored cell, as is suggested by that poem's subtly sinister tone and final admission that what was found in the world was only "myself."

By 1937 Stevens was positing a more complicated rela-
tionship between actor and stage. In section ix of "The Man
with the Blue Guitar" (CP, 169-70) the guitarist describes
himself in a blue landscape:

> And the color, the overcast blue
> Of the air, in which the blue guitar
>
> Is a form, described but difficult,
> And I am merely a shadow hunched
>
> Above the arrowy, still strings,
> The maker of a thing yet to be made;
>
> The color like a thought that grows
> Out of a mood, the tragic robe
>
> Of the actor, half his gesture, half
> His speech, the dress of his meaning, silk
>
> Sodden with his melancholy words,
> The weather of his stage, himself.

The primary meaning of this passage seems clearly to be that
the environment clothes and gives substance to the self, and
Stevens confirms this in his gloss:

> The imagination is not a free agent. It is not a faculty
> that functions spontaneously without references. In ix
> the reference is to environment: the overcast blue: the
> weather = the stage on which, in this instance, the
> imagination plays. The color of the weather is the role
> of the actor, which, after all, is a large part of him. The
> imagination depends on reality.   (L, 789)

Yet equally important is the countersuggestion that the setting
would have no meaning without the presence of the human
figure downstage. If we ask *whose* "thought that grows / Out
of a mood" the blue sky resembles, the answer can only be
"the actor's." If "the color of the weather" is "half his gesture,
half / His speech," the other half remains to be generated from

within. The open syntax of the final line upholds this inter-
dependence: the weather and the self are balanced against each
other on either side of the stage.

The final section of "The Man with the Blue Guitar" re-
states this resolution simply and beautifully. After insisting
that we must accept the things of this world as they are,
without evasion or denial, the guitarist asserts the proper place
for imagination:

> Here is the bread of time to come,
>
> Here is its actual stone. The bread
> Will be our bread, the stone will be
>
> Our bed and we shall sleep by night.
> We shall forget by day, except
>
> The moments when we choose to play
> The imagined pine, the imagined jay.
> (CP, 183-184)

We can become the world, can command the vision of a tree
or a bird, not through the monstrous egotism of Hoonian
solipsism, but through the exercise of imagination. Choice is
everything; by recognizing that we remain ourselves, actors
playing the role of pine or jay, we gain the double rewards of
experience and self-consciousness. As Stevens' mentor San-
tayana wrote, "I like the theater, not because I cannot perceive
that the play is a fiction, but because I do perceive it; if I
thought the thing a fact, I should detest it: anxiety would rob
me of all my imaginative pleasure."[10] Choosing to merge our
identity with the world's, yet insisting that such a merger is
fictive and temporary, we can maintain the essential awareness
of the self's integrity. In 1906 the young Stevens put it this
way: "There is a perfect rout of characters in every man—
and every man is like an actor's trunk, full of strange creatures,
new + old. But an actor and his trunk are two different
things" (L, 91). Frank Doggett's claim that "Stevens' sym-
bolic and anecdotal representations show that he feels the self

to be capable of infinite variations, of division into multiple selves, a chameleon of weather and feeling" would thus seem to be inaccurate. Seeing the self as "essentially protean, its old shape vanishing as the new is embodied in momentary attention,"[11] Doggett neglects the actual actor beneath the mask. Stevens might have countered, "The real is only the base. But it is the base" (OP, 160).

Stevens' fullest account of the response of the actor to "the weather of his stage" is "Of Modern Poetry" (CP, 239-40), which also provides an excellent model of the theater of the mind in which the reader is asked to participate. The poem dramatizes the moment when the mind must turn from the comfortable conventions of the past and confront the profoundly disordered world of the present. Several critics read the central image, the theater, as a symbol for the mind, "although the theater is much too vaguely defined to function very well as a true symbol. . . . Nonetheless, the objectifying of the mind as a theater does keep the poem from being purely philosophical or meditative."[12] In fact, the theater represents not the mind but the circumstances in which the mind finds itself. The shift from the old drama of memorized lines and predetermined scenic effects to the improvisational bare stage parallels the philosophical movement from religion to skepticism that is at the center of Stevens' work. Following one of his favorite procedures, the poem begins with an abstract proposition—"The poem of the mind in the act of finding / What will suffice"—and then pursues it through imaginative extensions that complicate and enliven the idea, so that it becomes "an abstraction blooded, as a man by thought" (CP, 385).

The voice of the poem thus speaks for the poet, but since it addresses the question of what kind of poetry needs to be written, it also speaks to him. His subject is both the modern mind and the modern poem, since for Stevens the two are ideally the same. The theater in which the actor finds himself requires not only that he speak lines his audience will understand, but that he invent them himself:

It has
To construct a new stage. It has to be on that stage
And, like an insatiable actor, slowly and
With meditation, speak words that in the ear,
In the delicatest ear of the mind, repeat,
Exactly, that which it wants to hear.

On this passage, Frank Lentricchia, Jr., comments:

The image that emerges is both grotesque and ironic.
The modern "poem of the mind" has suddenly stopped
its act of finding; has, in fact, abstracted from the par-
ticulars and constructed a "stage," a world. And on that
stage it stands, the modern poem, like a vain and pom-
pous actor, narcissistically gorging himself on all the
brilliant lines he can concoct, talking them somehow
into his own ear. The poem has moved to the position
that it implicitly rejects in its opening lines. . . . The
new romantic script has no idealistic framework, only
a huge egotistic motivation: the poem of the mind in
the act of finding becomes the poem of the mind in the
act of looking at itself and pronouncing the image good.[13]

I would argue that, although the image is wholly concerned
with the nature of self-fulfillment, it has nothing to do with
egotism. Stevens' actor appears on a stage deserted by play-
wright, director, and designer; if there is to be any drama, he
must invent it. His motivation is not narcissistic but an act
of faith; the text he produces is not "gorgeous nonsense" (NA,
3) but "the bread of faithful speech" (CP, 408). "The actor
is / A metaphysician in the dark," forced to depend on his
own ear because there is no external authority to whom he
can appeal. His goal is not merely self-approval, but "the
finding of a satisfaction," discovering words that will pass
"through sudden rightnesses" and satisfy, if only momentar-
ily, the rage for order.

Reading "Of Modern Poetry," we are, of course, the actor's
"invisible audience." But since the poem is not only about

writing poetry but about living in an age of disbelief, we play
the role of the actor as well. Stevens emphasizes this point by
saying that the audience, hearing the actor's words, "listens, /
Not to the play, but to itself," thus becoming actor and au-
dience at once. The entire movement of the poem is toward
this moment of creative fusion in the mind, "as of two people,
as of two / Emotions becoming one." The actor's sole re-
sponsibility—and by analogy, the poet's—is to discover the
text that will provoke this degree of imaginative sympathy,
which may draw upon the whole range of human activity:

> It must
> Be the finding of a satisfaction, and may
> Be of a man skating, a woman dancing, a woman
> Combing. The poem of the act of the mind.

"Of Modern Poetry" is constructed as a scenario of the kind
of text the modern "theater" requires; at the same time, it
furnishes us with an example of that text. It provides the
reader not with an idea but with the dramatized imaginative
experience of an idea, and concludes with precisely the sort
of emotional resolution it describes. The three figures of the
final lines are abstract illustrations of a concept, yet they are
also perfectly realizable images. The sense of the sentence
suggests that Stevens might have used any three verbs, but
clearly these are not random choices, since skating, dancing,
and combing reflect the combination of activity and solitude
that characterize the actor's performance. Imagining these fig-
ures, the reader completes the scenario, and in that act of the
mind discovers the sufficient theater the poem set out to find.

The search for an adequate theater is again central in "Rep-
etitions of a Young Captain" (CP, 306-10). From the confused
repetitions of his speech ("It was something overseas / That
I remembered, something that I remembered / Overseas"),
we sense that the captain has been deeply disturbed by his
wartime experiences. But the scene that is emblematic of his
confusion comes not from the battlefield but from the theater.
He tells us that once he was watching a performance in a

theater, when a violent storm "beat in the roof and half the walls." Suddenly theatrical illusion was shattered by a more astonishing reality:

It had been real. It was not now. The rip
Of the wind and the glittering were real now,
In the spectacle of a new reality.

Caught between the two poles, the audience remained motionless, "as if nothing had happened," and the actor on stage could only stand there, "glibly gapering. / Then faintly encrusted, a tissue of the moon / Walked toward him on the stage and they embraced." Real moonlight replaced the stage lighting, revealing it as artificial and antiquated, "like a machine left running, and running down." The landscape is exposed as a painted backdrop, "a blue scene washing white in the rain." The destruction of the theater, and thus of theatrical illusion, is analogous to the passing of the traditional theater in "Of Modern Poetry"; under the pressure of reality, the artificial stage conventions become too foreign and remote for the captain to believe in, and he must search for a more adequate mode of belief.

But that mode is not supplied either by the "calculated chaos" of war. The captain recognizes that warfare precipitates its own set of myths and abstractions, as artificial in its own way as the machinery of the stage:

. . . a giant sense
To the make-matter, matter-nothing mind,
.   .   .   .
An image that leaves nothing much behind.

He chooses instead to seek "his point between the two, / The organic consolation." Faced with a choice between a theater of total illusion, constructed from paint and "a beau language without a drop of blood," and the European Theater, which has no meaning beyond its own gigantic image, he chooses a third:

And if it be theatre for theatre,
The powdered personals against the giants' rage,
Blue and its deep inversions in the moon

Against gold whipped reddened in big-shadowed
    black,
Her vague "Secrete me from reality,"
His "That reality secrete itself,"

The choice is made. Green is the orator
Of our passionate height. He wears a tufted green,
And tosses green for those for whom green speaks.

In the green theater of reality, neither evaded nor inflated, the young captain finds speech sufficient "to bear with the exactest force / The precisions of fate." He learns that, as Stevens says in "The Auroras of Autumn," "there is no play. / Or, the persons act one merely by being here" (CP, 416). Crucially, Stevens does not suggest that the idea of theater itself is outmoded; he says simply that its language and action must be true to green reality:

Sordid Melpomene, why strut bare boards,
Without scenery or lights, in the theatre's bricks,
Dressed high in heliotrope's inconstant hue,

The muse of misery? Speak loftier lines,
Cry out, "I am the purple muse." Make sure
The audience beholds you, not your gown.
                                        (CP, 427)

Stevens' green theater, poised between pure imagination and pure reality, provides the stage on which most of his poems are acted out, particularly those of the final section of his *Collected Poems, The Rock*. Isabel G. MacCaffrey has pointed out the explicit references to *The Tempest* in the late poems, and noted the appropriateness of comparison between Stevens' work and Shakespeare's most profound exploration of the union of art and nature, a comparison we might profitably extend.[14] In "The Planet on the Table," Stevens wears the mask of Ariel, whose poems, "although makings of his self, / Were no less makings of the sun" (CP, 532). But if Stevens is Ariel, the protean shaping spirit of the imagination, he is also Prospero, the wise magus who controls Ariel, and who understands the necessity of returning from the enchanted island to the real world. His magic depends, as Prospero himself tells us, on the power of imagination, and requires an audience willing to give in to its spell; yet he takes great pains, again like Prospero, to reveal its theatrical, illusory nature. This self-conscious, open artifice inverts the classical image of the stage as a mirror of the audience, instead turning the world into a gigantic theater. Stevens' art, like Prospero's, depends for its effect on the willing participation of its audience. By itself it is only scenario, but in "the immensest theatre" of the reader's imagination it is brought to life: "the design of all his words takes form / And frame from thinking and is realized" (CP, 510-11).

Another recurrent image that helps to define the "right reader" of Stevens' poems is that of the reader and his book. Stevens was deeply interested in the alchemy of text, in the relationship between words on a page and the reader's power to enter and bring them to life; his exploration of this motif suggests, perhaps even more immediately than that of the theater, the active role he wanted his readers to play. One of the earliest poems based on this image is "The Reader" (CP, 146-47):

> All night I sat reading a book,
> Sat reading as if in a book
> Of sombre pages.   ,
>
> It was autumn and falling stars
> Covered the shrivelled forms
> Crouched in the moonlight.

No lamp was burning as I read,
A voice was mumbling, "Everything
Falls back to coldness, .

Even the musky muscadines,
The melons, the vermilion pears
Of the leafless garden."

The sombre pages bore no print
Except the trace of burning stars
In the frosty heaven.

The poem is a good deal more than the exercise in perception
(or in thermodynamics)[15] it may seem. Ingeniously, if with
excessive subtlety, the speaker creates a metaphor and si-
multaneously undermines it: he makes what seems a straight-
forward statement ("All night I sat reading a book"), then
reveals it to be metaphorical ("as if in a book": the book is
in fact a frosty autumnal universe), and in turn admits that
his metaphor applies only minimally ("No lamp was burning
as I read," "The sombre pages bore no print / Except the
trace of burning stars"). What is interesting about the poem
is, precisely, the role of the reader. The voice that mumbles,
"Everything / Falls back to coldness," thus revealing the book's
plot, must in this deserted landscape be the voice of the reader
himself. Just as the book is an image he projects onto the
leafless garden, the plot is the meaning he derives from it.
The book one must read in the dark, and the meaning of
whose faint print one must decipher alone, is thus analogous
to the bare, improvisational theater of the mind. The reader,
Stevens suggests, must bring his or her own illumination to
what is often a necessarily impoverished text.

"Phosphor Reading by His Own Light" (CP, 267) realizes
and extends this idea. Again, no lamp is burning. Phosphor
reads the dark page by virtue both of his own luminous prop-
erties and of knowing "what it is that he expects"—in short,
by anticipating the text before he encounters it. This causes
epistemological difficulties, since the text turns out not to

exist: "The page is blank or a frame without a glass / Or a glass that is empty when he looks." The mirror that appears to be empty may in fact reflect the blank white light of Phosphor's own reflection; in any case, it swallows up reality: "The greenness of night . . . goes / Down deeply in the empty glass." Although Frank Doggett sees Phosphor as both one who anticipates the future and a realist who "cannot know what specific word, what exact detail, to expect," and who thus both "knows and does not know what he expects,"[16] I tend to view the "realist" to whom the second half of the poem turns as a figure antithetical to Phosphor:

> Look, realist, not knowing what you expect.
> The green falls on you as you look,
>
> Falls on and makes and gives, even a speech.
> And you think that that is what you expect,
>
> That elemental parent, the green night,
> Teaching a fusky alphabet.

The realist who approaches the text without preconceptions is bathed in the creative green light of reality, which in turn begins to teach him a new language, the fusky alphabet of self-discovery. The right reader can expect, not to know what the page will say before he or she reads it, but to gain from the reading experience a heightened illumination of the world.

The distinction between "The Reader" who mumbles the plot of a book he has himself shaped from the bare landscape, and the phosphorescent reader who presumes to know the content of the unread page, is a narrow but crucial line. Reading a deeply impoverished text—whether it consists of a chilly landscape or the abstract meditation of a philosophical poet—must be undertaken in humility. Stevens' ideal reader realizes that to illuminate a text is not to confer on it one's own identity, or to fix its energies into rigid form. As in "The Idea of Order at Key West," the perception of order may become the creation of order, but the order must be recognized as fictive and temporary, and the text beyond the reading remains "the meaningless plungings of water and the wind" (CP, 129). The most a reader can hope to attain is a moment of vivid identity with the text, in which the differences between them seem to disappear. Stevens describes such a moment in "The House Was Quiet and the World Was Calm" (CP, 358-59):

> The house was quiet and the world was calm.
> The reader became the book; and summer night
>
> Was like the conscious being of the book.
> The house was quiet and the world was calm.
>
> The words were spoken as if there was no book,
> Except that the reader leaned above the page,
>
> Wanted to lean, wanted much most to be
> The scholar to whom his book is true, to whom
>
> The summer night is like a perfection of thought.
> The house was quiet because it had to be.
>
> The quiet was part of the meaning, part of the mind:
> The access of perfection to the page.
>
> And the world was calm. The truth in a calm world,
> In which there is no other meaning, itself
>
> Is calm, itself is summer and night, itself
> Is the reader leaning late and reading there.

The insistent repetitions, measured rhythms, and subtle shift from past to present tense draw the reader into an almost hypnotic trance in which the purely abstract description gains power and immediacy, and which is also "part of the meaning, part of the mind." At the same time, the reader is distanced from the poem by his or her conscious recognition of its self-reflexive nature; reading the poem, which seems to describe us in the act of reading, we are apt to be jarred out of the trance of identity the poem establishes. Asked to identify ourselves with the book in our hands, we grow paradoxically more aware of our separateness. This simultaneous movement, both sympathetically into the poem and self-consciously away from it, is paradigmatic of the double vision Stevens' poems so often evoke.

Despite its title, "Large Red Man Reading" (CP, 423-24) seems not to be about the reader, who is never described; the focus of the poem is on the band of ghosts who return "from the wilderness of stars" to earth. But the poem does seem to illuminate the reader's role, since—to confuse the matter further—the Large Red Man represents not the reader but the poet, while the reader of the poem stands in the position of the ghosts. This transfer is accompanied by an ambiguity of tone; though we are meant to feel sympathetic to the ghosts' need to regain contact with the poetry of earth, their passion for harsh reality seems, as in "Repetitions of a Young Captain," to risk over-inflation:

> They were those that would have wept to step
>   barefoot into reality,
>
> That would have wept and been happy, have
>   shivered in the frost
> And cried out to feel it again, have run fingers over
>   leaves
> And against the most coiled thorn, have seized on
>   what was ugly
>
> And laughed.

This intensity is obviously a measure of their desperation, but the large red man manages to fulfill their need in a more balanced and less melodramatic way: he bridges the gap "between fact and miracle" (OP, 232) through the medium of his imagination. His text is thus both physical reality and "the syllables of its law." Out of his "great blue tabulae," he reads not life but "the poem of life," not frost and thorns but "*poesis, poesis.*" The book is composed of both the commonplace ("the literal characters") and the visionary ("the vatic lines"); only in the combination can we find the text

Which in those ears and in those thin, those
    spended hearts,
Took on color, took on shape and the size of things
    as they are
And spoke the feeling for them, which was what
    they had lacked.

Here again the text alone will not suffice; only through the
medium of the reader's imagination does it spring to articulate
life.

But what exactly is the text the particular reader of Stevens
confronts? It is, of course, primarily lyric, and it is dramatic
in the complex and subtle way I have described. I would
suggest that it is also narrative. Most critics apparently believe
quite the opposite, that after the extended mock-epic of "The
Comedian as the Letter C," Stevens' interest in narrative waned
as his poetry grew more discursive and meditative. Helen
Vendler puts the case plainly: "The narrative progress was
deeply uncongenial to his mind, which moved always in ed-
dies, never in dramatic sequence. Stevens' tendency . . . is to
branch, to proliferate, to multiply, not to come to an end."[17]
But this position, like the view that Stevens' art is not dra-
matic, is founded on too narrow a generic definition. It ig-
nores the fact that often absorbing narratives—one thinks of
Cervantes, Sterne, Joyce, Borges—do not come to an end,
but multiply themselves endlessly in the reader's mind. Ste-
vens never wrote fully achieved, fixed narratives, which would
have violated his sense of experience as constant flux and
disorder; even "The Comedian" breaks off abruptly and in-
conclusively. Yet he repeatedly incorporated narrative ele-
ments into his poems, often with striking results.

Given his consuming interest in the act of imagination, in
the ways we transform our fragmented, chaotic existence into
patterns and myths of order, Stevens' attraction to the idea
of "the narrative progress" is not surprising. But realizing
that to construct a self-contained narrative poem would be to
evade his sense of reality, he had to find another way of

dramatizing "the more than rational distortion, / The fiction
that results from feeling" (CP, 406). His solution was to embed
fragments of narrative, often as "incidental" examples or par-
ables, within the context of lyric meditations. These frag-
ments do not simply function as examples, of course, but,
like Homeric similes, have their own compelling narrative
interest. And since they are often deeply ambiguous and in-
conclusive, tantalizingly suggestive of the complete fiction of
which they are only glimpses, the reader's sense of the frag-
mentary nature of our knowledge of existence is heightened:

> He was at Naples writing letters home
> And, between his letters, reading paragraphs
> On the sublime. Vesuvius had groaned
> For a month.
>
> (CP, 313)

> This is the chair from which she gathered up
> Her dress, the carefulest, commodious weave
>
> Inwoven by a weaver to twelve bells . . .
> The dress is lying, cast-off, on the floor.
>
> (CP, 428)

> A car drives up. A soldier, an officer,
> Steps out. He rings and knocks. The door is
>   not locked.
> He enters the room and calls. No one is there.
>
> (CP, 452)

While these poems may be frustrating to the wholly rational
critic, they are also extraordinarily stimulating; they tempt us
to reinvent the whole from the part. Stevens means to expose
his reader to the liberating pleasures of the fictive imagination,
without neatly closing off that experience. The result is, in
the most effective poems, to draw the reader directly into the
fictional process. As Randall Jarrell says, "In narrative at its
purest or most eventful we do not understand but are the
narrative. When we understand completely (or laugh com-

pletely, or feel completely a lyric empathy with the beings of
the world), the carrying force of the narrative is dissipated:
in fiction, to understand everything is to get nowhere."[18]

A little-known poem that describes this process and is at
the same time an example of it is the one briefly introduced
in my preface, "A Golden Woman in a Silver Mirror" (CP,
460–61):

> Suppose this was the root of everything.
> Suppose it turned out to be or that it touched
> An image that was mistress of the world.
>
> For example: Au Château. Un Salon. A glass
> The sun steps into, regards and finds itself;
> Or: Gawks of hay . . . Augusta Moon, before
>
> An attic glass, hums of the old Lutheran bells
> At home; or: In the woods, belle Belle alone
> Rattles with fear in unreflecting leaves.
>
> Abba, dark death is the breaking of a glass.
> The dazzled flakes and splinters disappear.
> The seal is as relaxed as dirt, perdu.
>
> But the images, disembodied, are not broken.
> They have, or they may have, their glittering crown,
> Sound-soothing pearl and omni-diamond,
>
> Of the most beautiful, the most beautiful maid
> And mother. How long have you lived and looked,
> Ababba, expecting this king's queen to appear?

The poem begins and ends with an hypothesis that stands
Plato on his head: suppose apparently illusory images—both
in the mirror and in the imagination—had an independent
existence that transcended the reality they supposedly re-
flected. Stevens promptly realizes this idea, inventing exam-
ples that in their broadly parodic texture and extravagantly
novelistic language go far beyond mere illustration. He erects
a wilderness of mirrors, of which the two most important are

the poet's imagination (in which hypothesis finds "concrete" reflection) and the reader's (which reflects the object that is the poem, and brings it to life). He then shatters the mirrors, thus severing the images' connection with reality, and stands back to observe the proof of his hypothesis: "the images, disembodied, are not broken." Augusta Moon and belle Belle do not dissolve, but remain vivid in the reader's mind, even when we have watched them shatter before our eyes. And the disembodied idea of the golden woman remains so potent for the shadowy Ababba that he stands transfixed before the empty frame, awaiting her return. This is all "the sense of the sleight-of-hand man" (CP, 222), of course; Stevens' delighted confusion of reality and realized illusion is witty and dazzling. Yet the poem is solidly based on his ideas of perception, belief, and the necessary angel of the imagination in a skeptical age.

Stevens' most remarkable treatment of the relation between reader and narrative text, "The Novel" (CP, 457-59), has been almost totally neglected, and the one extended discussion seriously distorts its meaning. James Baird calls the poem "the last of Stevens' full projections in masque form. . . . Present reality was never asserted more forcefully by Stevens than here. It is a reality of 1948; and it is a reality of advancing age."[19] Armed with the evidence that Stevens borrowed one passage verbatim from one of his correspondents, he goes on to imply that the poem stands in clear and stable relation to "reality," and that from knowledge of that reality its meaning can be derived. This is to neglect the reader's experience of the poem, which is deeply mysterious and elusive, a constant collapsing of reality into illusion.

"The Novel" begins by describing the natural landscape in terms of artifice:

The crows are flying above the foyer of summer.
The winds batter it. The water curls. The leaves
Return to their original illusion.

From this landscape an unidentified "he" is departing, leaving
the fictive "foyer of summer" for "the rodomontadean emp-
tiness . . . of the past." Then follows an italicized passage
whose relation to the landscape seems unclear:

> *Mother was afraid I should freeze in the Parisian hotels.*
> *She had heard of the fate of an Argentine writer. At night,*
> *He would go to bed, cover himself with blankets—*
>
> *Protruding from the pile of wool, a hand,*
> *In a black glove, holds a novel by Camus. She begged*
> *That I stay away.* These are the words of José . . .

> He is sitting by the fidgets of a fire,
> The first red of red winter, winter-red,
> The late, least foyer in a qualm of cold.

> How tranquil it was at vividest Varadero.

At this point, through a process of reconstruction, the reader
can piece together the content of the fiction: José, the "he"
of the second stanza, has at his mother's behest left Paris and
returned to Varadero. But this "plot" does not account for
the mysterious effects of the narration: the collapsing of time
into one continuous present, the bizarre, surrealistic image of
the Argentine writer, the uncertain relation of the narrator to
José. José has traveled from the energetic landscape of Paris
to a scene preternaturally composed:

> But here tranquillity is what one thinks.
> The fire burns as the novel taught it how.

> The mirror melts and moulds itself and moves
> And catches from nowhere brightly-burning breath.
> It blows a glassy brightness on the fire

> And makes flame flame and makes it bite the wood
> And bite the hard-bite, barking as it bites.
> The arrangement of the chairs is so and so,

> Not as one would have arranged them for oneself,
> But in the style of the novel.

In such meditative tranquillity, the poem becomes almost completely self-reflexive. As in "A Golden Woman," the fictive reflections gain dominance and force "reality" to conform to them; "the thing imagined is the imaginer" (OP, 178). The novel that teaches the fire how to burn may be the book José is reading, or the Camus novel he remembers from his mother's story, or "The Novel" which encloses both José and the fire, and in which they are equally fictive.

As José finishes his book, the distinctions imposed by narrative disappear, so that the reader who has entered the poem finds himself sharing the consciousness of both José and the poet:

> Day's arches are crumbling into the autumn night.
> The fire falls a little and the book is done.
> The stillness is the stillness of the mind.
>
> Slowly the room grows dark. It is odd about
> That Argentine. Only the real can be
> Unreal today, be hidden and alive.

And in one further turn of the imaginative screw, we are forced into the mind of the Argentine, that real unreal we have not been able to forget:

> It is odd, too, how that Argentine is oneself,
> Feeling the fear that creeps beneath the wool,
> Lies on the breast and pierces into the heart,
>
> Straight from the Arcadian imagination,
> Its being beating heavily in the veins,
> Its knowledge cold within one as one's own;
>
> And one trembles to be so understood and, at last,
> To understand, as if to know became
> The fatality of seeing things too well.

Asked at the beginning of the poem to construct the narrative, then to share its dissolution into self-consciousness, the reader must now evaluate that experience. As the last veil of fiction is drawn aside, we become both ourselves and the Argentine, both reader and text. As the Argentine, huddled in the dark, cold room, we face the terrible, impoverished knowledge of being stripped of all illusions, "the fatality of seeing things too well." Yet our self-consciousness reminds us that even this identification results from the fictive fire of "the Arcadian imagination"; "the absence of the imagination had / Itself to be imagined" (CP, 503). "The Novel" engages us through the action of our own imaginations in an experience deeply mimetic of the ways our identities are bound up in the fictions we conceive. To see the fiction simultaneously from inside and out, "to be so understood and, at last, / To understand," is to experience for a moment that sublime "degree of perception at which what is real and what is imagined are one" (OP, 166).

3
The Motive for Metaphor

> There was a will to change, a necessitous
> And present way, a presentation, a kind
> Of volatile world, too constant to be denied,
>
> The eye of a vagabond in metaphor
> That catches our own.
>
> Stevens, "Notes Toward a Supreme Fiction"

> A. A violent order is disorder; and
> B. A great disorder is an order. These
> Two things are one. (Pages of illustrations.)
>
> (CP, 215)

Given their persistent need to seek sources of meaning and coherence in individual acts of imagination, modern poets have been acutely aware of a paradoxical problem: how to present a shifting, dynamic world without distortion in a work of art that is to some degree necessarily fixed and static. The important formal experiments in the literature—as, indeed, in all the arts—of this century may be seen as attempts to mediate between the perception that "Life is Motion" (CP, 83) and the "blessed rage for order." Stevens' response to this problem was to write poems that represent both the mirror and the lamp, poems that are radically mimetic of the world of process and at the same time are given illumination and perspective by the shaping spirit of the poet's imagination.

To do this, his transparent lyrics focus increasingly often, not on the concrete images of the world, but on the mind in the act of reaching for and responding to those images. From about 1940, Stevens' primary means for figuring these acts of imagination rhetorically is to make the act of metaphorical thinking itself the subject of the poem.

In discussing the acts of the mind embodied in Stevens' poems, Louis Martz draws our attention to "the inexhaustible 'realm of resemblance,' in which the faculties of the imagination, using all their powers, 'extend the object' by analogy, by metaphor. . . . By the use of such analogies man connects the external and the internal; the action of analogy is the mind's ultimate way of establishing its dominant, controlling position amid the 'moving chaos that never ends.' "[1] Similarly, Joseph Riddel's analysis of the early poems suggests that in them Stevens attempts to relate "himself to his world by ingesting its flow of appearances and transforming sensation into the rhythms and forms of his own sensibility."[2] Such views seem to indicate that Stevens' theory and practice conform to the Romantics' confidence in the metamorphic power of metaphor, as expressed most clearly in Shelley's *Defence of Poetry*:

> [Poets'] language is vitally metamorphical; that is, it marks the before unapprehended relations of things and perpetuates their apprehension until the words which represent them become, through time, signs for portions or classes of thoughts instead of pictures of integral thoughts. . . . Language itself is poetry; and to be a poet is to apprehend the true and the beautiful.[3]

But careful examination of Stevens' remarks about metaphor in his notebooks reveals a considerably more complex and divided position, a sense of ironic possibilities that anticipates postmodernism. Sometimes he appears, like the Romantics, to affirm the imagination's ability actually to reshape the order of the world through language:

The imagination is man's power over nature. (OP, 179)

Metaphor creates a new reality from which the original appears to be unreal. (OP, 169)

Reality is a cliché from which we escape by metaphor. It is only *au pays de la métaphore qu'on est poète.* (OP, 179)

At other times he expresses the primacy of reality:

Eventually an imaginary world is entirely without interest. (OP, 175)

Reality is the spirit's true center. (OP, 177)

Critics have often taken such apparent inconsistency as evidence of Stevens' capitulation to dualism. For example, Suzanne Juhasz writes, "Although Stevens's definitions of metaphor alter little in the various statements that he makes about it, his evaluation of it does change radically. Sometimes he thinks of it as evil, sometimes as salvation."[4] Similarly, Roy Harvey Pearce at one time argued that in the late poems Stevens actually moves toward affirming the separation between mind and matter:

The poems may move toward one of two ends: toward celebrating the power of the subject, the mind which not only wills but makes its knowledge; or toward celebrating the givenness of the object, the reality which is unchanging and unchangeable, perdurably out there. . . . The utopian alternatives are pure introspection and pure abstraction—knowledge of pure act as against knowledge of pure substance.[5]

But though Pearce is correct in identifying "the radical disjunction . . . between act and substance"[6] as the central problem for Stevens, I believe he is wrong to suggest that the poet ever abandons the "attempt to bridge the gap between fact and miracle" (OP, 232), between the thing itself and metaphorical transformation of it. The notion of the supreme fiction depends on the constant dialectical movement between them.[7] The seasonal terms in which Stevens most often represents the poles of belief emphasize their opposition; just as it cannot be both summer and winter at once, the absolute merger of self and object is never possible. But the pure objectivity of "The Snow Man" and the total subjectivity of "Credences of Summer" are states that exist only momentarily before beginning to swing back toward their opposites. Winter is always "devising summer in its breast" (CP, 186). And in the particular strategy of the transparent lyric Stevens found a way to represent this dialectic dramatically.

Stevens' theory of metaphor depends in part on his free use of the word "reality" in two different ways, which has in turn confused discussions of the matter. Helen Regueiro's recent discussion of metaphor in Stevens, for example, is grounded in a sense of opposition between the immediate reality of an object and the metaphor that is "an artifice that cannot take hold in reality."[8] But although he was content to posit for the sake of discussion a realm of pure objectivity, Stevens throughout his career affirmed that we cannot know objects except through our imaginative perception of them: "things seen are things as seen" (OP, 162). "What our eyes behold may well be the text of life but one's meditations on the text and the disclosures of these meditations are no less a part of the structure of reality" (NA, 76). This more complex and vital reality emerges from the intersection of subject with object, and depends on the integrating act of metaphorical vision. Thus, although Stevens' sense of metaphor is deeply paradoxical, Joseph Riddel's claim that metaphor "evades and averts, and the poet finds evasion and averting both necessary and inadequate"[9] would seem to be inaccurate. Rather, the action of metaphor is both an evasion of "reality" in the purely objective sense and the means of approaching the more vital "reality" we can experience. "Reality is not what it is. It consists of the many realities which it can be made into" (OP, 178). Far from simply quixotic, Stevens' stress on the two kinds of reality here is crucial to his understanding of metaphor. In reading the poems based on this understanding, we must learn to cultivate sensitivity to the way they enact a play of mind between the two poles.

Regueiro cites "Poem Written at Morning" (CP, 219) to demonstrate the view that "poetic metaphors are the divisive elements between the poet and reality."[10] The poem is presented not as a straightforward statement, as Regueiro's discussion might imply, but as mimetic of a fluid and transparent process of thought, and its meaning inheres not in discursive argument but in the reader's experience of that process.

> A sunny day's complete Poussiniana
> Divide it from itself. It is this or that
> And it is not.
>   By metaphor you paint
>   A thing.

The "complete Poussiniana" are presumably the painterly images by which the day may be represented. Reading the first line, we experience them as an integral part of the day. Not until the second line is there a sense of division or opposition. Moreover, this division is peculiar: not "pure" day on the one hand and Poussiniana on the other, but the day itself divided by its own images. "It is this or that" (as represented by a given image) "And it is not"—which may mean either that the image is a false representation, or that it is accurate but incomplete (because it is only one element of the complete Poussiniana), or that the image exists only fleetingly (it *is*, and then it is *not*). At any rate, the poem's ambiguity to this point prevents the reader from extracting a didactic statement from it. Regueiro's claim that "through the metaphor the object is posed into 'this' or 'that'—always into something that violates its 'thingness.' . . . The painting of metaphor is ultimately a faking of reality, not a valid means of experiencing it"[11] incorporates a judgment of value that the poem itself does not support. In fact, the poem goes on to suggest that metaphor is not only valid but the *only* means of experiencing reality; what had been a rather oblique and difficult abstraction shifts into a wonderfully evocative series of images:

> Thus, the pineapple was a leather fruit,
> A fruit for pewter, thorned and palmed and blue,
> To be served by men of ice.
> The senses paint
> By metaphor. The juice was fragranter
> Than wettest cinnamon. It was cribled pears
> Dripping a morning sap.

Surely this kind of painting is no mere whitewash but a provision of essential shape and color. The shift into past tense is a fine touch, suggesting that metaphor provides not only imaginative substance but narrative context and perspective. It is, of course, in a sense a "violation," since in being painted the object becomes less "pure," but its necessity is suggested by the fact that the pineapple does not appear in the poem until it is represented by the metaphor. And the action of metaphor is not the static portraiture suggested by Regueiro's term "posed"; the poem enacts a fluid and playful metamorphosis, leather fruit through blue palms and wettest cinnamon to cribled pears. Through the action of metaphor we manage not only to see the pineapple more clearly and vividly, but also to unite the various parts of its world.

Finally, the poem moves back toward generalization, toward the perception that "what we see in the mind is as real to us as what we see by the eye" (OP, 162):

> The truth must be
> That you do not see, you experience, you feel,
> That the buxom eye brings merely its element
> To the total thing, a shapeless giant forced
> Upward.
> Green were the curls upon that head.

The resources of the imagination's Poussiniana are apparently endless, and no one image can suffice to paint a thing. If the pineapple can be both a leather fruit and a green-curled head, then clearly metaphor prevents us from ever reaching "pure" pineapple; on the other hand, without metaphor—without imaginative comparison to other things we know—we could never experience pineapple at all. The dialectic of "Poem Written at Morning" does not come to any neat synthetic close; its meaning remains implicit except as the reader himself or herself arrives at it. Understanding the poem is not a matter of interpreting what it *says*, but of seeing the world in terms of its particular associative vision. Its effect is strikingly similar to that of the following passage from a 1942 letter: "When a poet makes his imagination the imagination of other people, he does so by making them see the world through his eyes. Most modern activity is the undoing of that very job. The world has been painted; most modern activity is getting rid of the paint to get at the world itself" (L, 402). A reading like Regueiro's emphasizes the idea of the second half of this passage, and implies that the poet's responsibility is to get rid of the paint. But understanding Stevens' theory of metaphor requires accepting both sides of the balance he establishes. The poet both paints the world—by making readers see the world through his own buxom eye—and unpaints it, and neither pole is any more "fake" or "real" than summer or winter is.

For Stevens there are two kinds of metaphor. On the one hand, there are what Riddel calls "the forced penetrations of metaphor,"[12] willful assertions of resemblance that remain merely rhetorical. On the other hand, there is a kind of vital metaphor that actually changes the world by changing the way we see it. The difference is that of authenticity: the first attempts to *impose* patterns of resemblance on the world, while the second seeks out and reveals relations that are recognized as true. Any "man of imagination," Stevens tells us, forms the "habit of the mind by which it probes for an integration" (OP, 196), while for the poet the motive for metaphor finds specifically verbal expression, but in each case the motive is the same: "to change nature, not merely to change ideas"

(CP, 234). Stevens makes clear that such metamorphosis is
not only not evasive, but necessary:

> The freshness of transformation is
>
> The freshness of a world. It is our own,
> It is ourselves, the freshness of ourselves,
> And that necessity and that presentation
>
> Are rubbings of a glass in which we peer.
> (CP, 397–98)

Imaginative perception is for Stevens essential to self-defini-
tion and self-renewal.

The relation between the two kinds of metaphor is the
subject of "Bouquet of Roses in Sunlight" (CP, 430–31), which
is often taken as evidence of Stevens' ultimate dismissal of
metaphor.[13] The opening of the poem indeed seems to suggest
as much; the bold actuality of the bouquet resists any imag-
inative transformation:

> Say that it is a crude effect, black reds,
> Pink yellows, orange whites, too much as they are
> To be anything else in the sunlight of the room,
>
> Too much as they are to be changed by metaphor,
> Too actual, things that in being real
> Make any imaginings of them lesser things.

Yet this is followed by the recognition that such apparently
immediate reality is mediated by our individual perception of
it. The vivid colors have impact only with reference to our
prior associations with them—in other words, only as they
are given metaphorical contexts in our act of perception:

> And yet this effect is a consequence of the way
> We feel and, therefore, is not real, except
> In our sense of it, our sense of the fertilest red,
>
> Of yellow as first color and of white,
> In which the sense lies still, as a man lies,
> Enormous, in a completing of his truth.

Thus, although the word "metaphor" refers in this poem to
superficial and rhetorical metamorphosis, the internalized
"sense" of the roses incorporates the metaphorical "activity
of resemblance" (NA, 77) Stevens often described. As in "Poem
Written at Morning," the difference is between seeing and
experiencing: "The eye does not beget in resemblance. It sees.
But the mind begets in resemblance as the painter begets in
representation; that is to say, as the painter makes his world
within a world" (NA, 76). This idea emerges not through
discursive argument, but in the way in which the poem's
rhetoric evokes a shifting sensibility:

> Our sense of these things changes and they change,
> Not as in metaphor, but in our sense
> Of them. So sense exceeds all metaphor.
>
> It exceeds the heavy changes of the light.
> It is like a flow of meanings with no speech
> And of as many meanings as of men.
>
> We are two that use these roses as we are,
> In seeing them. This is what makes them seem
> So far beyond the rhetorician's touch.

As the poem moves toward clearer discrimination between
mere rhetoric and imaginative vision, the presentation of the
bouquet of roses shifts from a two-dimensional, painterly
sensation of color ("a crude effect, black reds, / Pink yellows
. . .") to objects important not for what they appear but for
what they mean ("of as many meanings as of men"). The
flowers become a medium for the communication of feeling,
operating—like the poem itself—not through rational dis-
course but through experience ("a flow of meanings with no
speech"). So too the rhetoric of the poem deepens from the
impersonal hypothesis of the opening ("Say that it is a crude
effect") to the surprising last stanza, which seems to implicate
the reader directly in the equation of being and seeing ("We
are two that use these roses as we are, / In seeing them").
For a moment the poem becomes a demonstration of the way

in which feeling is evoked not by discourse but by the experience of imagination.

Perpetuated by memory and convention, even the most vital and compelling metaphors grow stale. Mythologies lose their imaginative potency, poetic neologisms turn cliché, the names of constellations fill "a junk-shop, / Full of javelins and old fire-balls, / Triangles and the names of girls" (CP, 218). (This last is, of course, a brilliant metaphor, itself evidence of Stevens' double view.) When metaphors are no longer fresh and vivid, they have outlived their usefulness and must be discarded. Through a process of radical skepticism we return to what Stevens calls the first idea: to "see the very thing and nothing else" (CP, 373). Yet he makes clear that even while we are stripping away old metaphors, our perception of the world necessarily remains imaginative and mediate:

> To say the solar chariot is junk
>
> Is not a variation but an end.
> Yet to speak of the whole world as meta-
>   phor
> Is still to stick to the contents of the mind
>
> And the desire to believe in a metaphor.
> It is to stick to the nicer knowledge of
> Belief, that what it believes in is not true.
>   (CP, 332)

A number of critics fail to see that Stevens' winter vision is only part of his cycle of belief. For example, while recognizing rightly that for Stevens "the poetic illusion is . . . not a penetration to a more deeply interfused ontological structure," Frank Lentricchia also maintains that "Stevens does not hold that metaphor is a valid way of understanding reality."[14] Without acknowledging Stevens' complex use of "metaphor" and "reality," he continues:

> Given that reality is self-existent and self-explanatory, man's symbolic forms do not, obviously, constitute it.

Reality has fully formed, independent attributes prior
to our perception of it; truth is objective, inherent in the
self-existing real; and the best thing we can do to per-
ceive truth is to neutralize the individuality of our per-
spectives. . . . Stevens . . . believed that cognition was
a scientific value and not an aesthetic one.[15]

Lentricchia's naturalistic stance, however familiar, seems to
me to misread Stevens' position. In claiming that we can
engage the real only by neutralizing our subjective percep-
tions, he makes the same mistake as the "floribund ascetic"
who is the subject of "Landscape with Boat" (CP, 241-43).
Stevens' "anti-master man" also feels a deep mistrust of met-
aphor, and pursues the quest for the truth that he thinks lies
beyond all colors and images:

> He wanted imperceptible air.
> He wanted to see. He wanted the eye to see
> And not be touched by blue . . .
> . . . Nabob
> Of bones, he rejected, he denied, to arrive
> At the neutral centre, the ominous element,
> The single-colored, colorless, primitive.

The irony is that without metaphor there is no truth to per-
ceive, or at least no self to perceive it. The "floribund ascetic"
implicitly fails to find "the neutral centre," and a more au-
thoritative voice emerges to suggest an inclusive view:

> He never supposed divine
> Things might not look divine, nor that if nothing
> Was divine then all things were, the world itself,
> And that if nothing was the truth, then all
> Things were the truth, the world itself was the truth.

The poem as a whole might be taken as clear refutation of
the attempt to see scientifically rather than aesthetically.

At the same time, "Landscape with Boat" is not simply
didactic; as is characteristic in the transparent lyric, the rhetoric
brings the reader's own discrimination into play. In the pas-

sage just quoted, what might have been a straightforward
reversal of the nabob's expectations is couched instead, as
Helen Vendler notes, in hypothetical, conjectural terms.[16] Un-
der the microscope, the language squirms. We are not even
told that the nabob fails to find the truth, merely that "It was
not as if the truth lay where he thought." Moreover, the final
lines of the poem shift the reader's perspective radically: what
has been a rather abstract parable becomes a vividly realized—
if still hypothetical—anecdote:

> Had he been better able to suppose:
> He might sit on a sofa on a balcony
> Above the Mediterranean, emerald
> Becoming emeralds. He might watch the palms
> Flap green ears in the heat. He might observe
> A yellow wine and follow a steamer's track
> And say. "The thing I hum appears to be
> The rhythm of this celestial pantomime."

The shift from past to present tense, and from abstractions
to concrete images, is significant: if the world itself is the
truth, then the more immediately we experience it, the closer
we are to truth. The "Landscape with Boat" is no longer a
painting on the wall but a scene invested with activity and
sensation, into which the reader is imaginatively catapulted.
While the narrative form of this poem differs from the char-
acteristic form of the transparent lyric as I have defined it, it
makes essentially the same demands. As the poem moves
rhetorically from description to hypostatized rejection to dra-
matic but still hypothetical speculation, the reader is forced
to decide what this movement means. The poem makes no
overt statement, yet at the same time it requires the reader to
judge that the world itself is the truth, to wish that the nabob
had been better able to suppose, to affirm that one's random
tune may echo the rhythm of the universe. The experience
of the poem, in other words, forces the reader to exercise
imagination and discrimination in order to discover its mean-
ing.

The notion of transparence, of a rhetoric that establishes its own incompleteness and requires the reader's active participation to achieve its meaning, would seem to exclude conventional uses of irony, which depends on a coherent and fully determined dramatic perspective. For this reason I find Helen Vendler's consistently ironic reading of Stevens' language, while more subtle than Lentricchia's dismissal of metaphor, often unconvincing. In fact, it is sometimes expressed in terms much like Lentricchia's, as in the following:

> Despair, in the flat poems, prompts not only the denial of the gaiety of language, but also a denial of the validity of metaphor. The natural world wears masks; and as we are reduced to simile, all we can do is "To say of one mask it is like, / To say of another it is like." The old tendency to metaphor, and to its poetic corollary the pathetic fallacy, dies hard, but it must grudgingly be suppressed, and only the simile, with its Gradgrind insistence on the unmagical, can be permitted.[17]

Vendler's reply to the hypothetical language of the poem—"He might observe / A yellow wine and follow a steamer's track"—would probably be, "On the other hand, he might not." Her sense of irony extends Stevens' supposed attitude toward metaphor into his very grammar, which often acquires significantly dark overtones: "When Stevens is reluctant to assert even an equivocal present or future, he resorts to hypothesis and supposition, chiefly by using his indispensable hypothetical 'if,' which takes away with one hand what the poet has already given with the other. . . . These 'ifs' of uncommitted assertion serve as points from which Stevens can suspend long deductions, making us disregard the shaky status of the antecedent." This view seems to me inadequate. It follows from judging poems according to Romantic conceptions of poetry as expressive "assertions," with the assumption that if a poet fails to make an unqualified assertion it is a sign of "unsatisfied desire."[18] In seeing a poem as transparent we may judge that its hypotheses and possibilities, rather than

expressing the poet's own anxieties or frustrations, serve in-
stead to establish a dialectical network, deliberately unre-
solved, which it is up to the reader to fulfill.

Thus in one poem Vendler finds "the constraint, the sad-
ness, the attempts at self-conviction, the wishful longing" all
conveyed by the subjective mood. To say that " 'seems' in-
troduces the uncertainty of knowledge, the likelihood of de-
ception, the possible quicksand of nature"[19] is to ignore the
playful, improvisational quality of Stevens' use of the hy-
pothetical, and to fail to see that for Stevens skepticism (which
Vendler typically calls "uncertainty") is a necessary condition
of free, creative thought. On what I take as one of Stevens'
most moving explorations of the paradox of belief—

> To discover winter and know it well, to find,
> Not to impose, not to have reasoned at all,
> Out of nothing to have come on major weather,
>
> It is possible, possible, possible: It must
> Be possible.
>
> (CP, 404)

she comments, "The mood of uncertainty in Stevens, whether
marked by direct questions or by implicit qualification, some-
times yields to a mood of desperate assertion, where a pas-
sionate insistence is based on fear, a fear of a dreadful disin-
tegration if the assertions prove false. . . . 'Must' is not a
word of faith but a word of doubt, implying as it does an
unbearable alternative."[20] The tone seems to me based neither
on desperation nor on fear but on hope. As Harold Bloom
says, "Repetitive and accumulative the rhetoric certainly is
here, but it is too controlled to be hysterical, and Stevens is
too shrewd and too sure of himself, at this point, to be des-
perate. He *is* overinsistent, because he is arguing against his
own reductiveness, but his insistence is on the possibility of
a middle path between reduction and expansion."[21] Stevens
is enough of a realist to recognize that knowledge of the
world, and the self-knowledge that ensues from it, cannot be

taken for granted or manufactured. At the same time, he insists passionately that such moments of conjunction can occur spontaneously, through sudden rightnesses, and that this *must* be possible—for surely "must" may be as much a word of faith as of doubt—if any integration or wholeness is to be achieved. At any rate it seems clear that Vendler does not take into account the *dramatic* aspect of the poems, the possibility that they are intended not simply to express the poet's "qualified assertions," but to evoke a complicated dialectical response in the reader. That this is an integral—I would say the essential—aspect of the poems may be seen by examining four poems from the 1940s, each of which deals specifically with the question of metaphor.

In naming a poem "The Motive for Metaphor" (CP, 288), Stevens leads us to expect that it will move in a more or less straightforward way toward a definition or description of that motive. But this expectation is thwarted; the poem explores its subject indirectly, dialectically, dramatically:

> You like it under the trees in autumn,
> Because everything is half dead.
> The wind moves like a cripple among the leaves
> And repeats words without meaning.
>
> In the same way, you were happy in spring,
> With the half colors of quarter-things,
> The slightly brighter sky, the melting clouds,
> The single bird, the obscure moon—
>
> The obscure moon lighting an obscure world
> Of things that would never be quite expressed,
> Where you yourself were never quite yourself
> And did not want nor have to be,
>
> Desiring the exhilarations of changes:
> The motive for metaphor, shrinking from
> The weight of primary noon,
> The A B C of being,

> The ruddy temper, the hammer
> Of red and blue, the hard sound—
> Steel against intimation—the sharp flash,
> The vital, arrogant, fatal, dominant X.

The characteristically oblique opening exemplifies the strategies of the transparent lyric. We cannot tie the voice to any dramatized speaker, nor can we identify its audience with any precision.[22] The lack of a referent for "it" in the first line is also a typical strategy, for it immediately engages the reader in the attempt to locate the referent and place it dramatically in the poem. Reading the first line, we are apt to take its "you" as a general address to the reader; if we think we are being told simply that we enjoy a pastoral scene, we acquiesce. But the rest of the stanza sharply qualifies this acceptance: the scene we like is revealed as a dying landscape through which the wind moves like an inarticulate cripple. And as the landscape grows darker and more sinister, the frame of reference for the "you" becomes smaller and more personal, and the claim that is being made about the "you" more acute. What seemed a generally applicable description of seasonal pleasure becomes a psychological judgment in which the reader is directly implicated. The judgment is so private that the "you" becomes a form of self-address, establishing a peculiarly internal quality that continues throughout the poem. Caught between the "you" of direct address and the "you" of self-recognition, we experience what the poem "says" from a strikingly self-conscious position.

If we have been jarred by the first stanza, the one following is more comforting. Our parallel pleasure in spring convinces us that our liking for autumn is based not on some morbid masochism but on the sheer experience of nature in transition from one pole to another. The images of spring are considerably less dark than those of autumn, but they have in common what Stevens elsewhere calls "the freshness of transformation" (CP, 397): "half colors" are thus parallel to "half dead." The motive for metaphor, the poem seems to be telling us, is the urge to achieve this transitional, metaphoric state, to catch one "reality" in the act of shifting into another. And yet this does not account for the total experience of the poem; its subtle emotional texture deepens and complicates the idea. The final image of spring, "the obscure moon," is not simply an emblem of transformation—as, for example, the moon's first or last quarter might be—but primarily one of uncertainty or mystery, paralleling the wind's meaningless words in the first stanza. The first two stanzas appear to be making a logical statement of definition, but beneath the surface is an essential core of mystery. Characteristically, the mental action embodied in the poem reflects this complexity: the forward progress is interrupted by the mind in meditation, which catches on this detail ("the obscure moon") and repeats it.

The extraordinary stanza that follows is completely ignored by every discussion of the poem I have seen. The obscure world lit by the obscure moon is more than a simple extension of the spring in halftones, more than an example of transition from one clearly defined pole to another. Rather, it is an inner landscape where the outlines of the self are blurred, and where objects and emotions are inevitably out of reach. The whole notion of fixed poles is thus called into question, and the compulsion toward stable identity is displaced by "the exhilarations of changes." This scene suggests that the motive for metaphor is not simply to enjoy an external scene in motion but to approach a state free from the order and clarity of self-expression, to reach a condition where language loses its customary meaning, the light we see by is uncertain, and identity is radically unstable—in other words, to change the self that sees as well as the way it sees.

The ending of the poem puts this principle into action, forcing us to see an image different from the one it ostensibly paints. The last two stanzas provide the definition we have expected since the title. As usual, Stevens' syntax is tricky, but it seems probable that we are to read "The motive for metaphor is [to shrink] from the weight of primary noon." The list that follows, apparently in apposition to "primary

noon," defines the world of fixed identities from which met-
aphor serves to liberate us. But the description departs from
the idea it seems intended to demonstrate. Paradoxically, the
images of this world are defined entirely *through* metaphors:
noon has weight, being is an alphabet, temper is ruddy, and
so on. Supposedly lacking "the exhilarations of changes," the
world of primary noon is full of action, producing hard sounds
and sharp flashes as concrete steel strikes against abstract in-
timation. And in claiming that "X is the enigma of reality
not contained in metaphor,"[23] Helen Regueiro misses the par-
adox that X is in algebra the ultimate metaphor, never quite
itself and always ready to assume another identity. In the final
line, X stands for reality but is itself a metaphor. Moreover,
in reading the line, we are forced by each adjective to revise
our shifting impression of X. The reality for which X stands
never appears; it is pure metaphor, protean X itself, that dom-
inates. The progress of the poem is thus not toward simple
definition, but toward that complex and mysterious experi-
ence it is the motive of metaphor to reveal.

"Metaphor as Degeneration" (CP, 444-45) shares with "The
Motive for Metaphor" an abstract title that has led some critics
to reduce the poem to an idea.[24] Again this is misleading;
"metaphor as degeneration" is not the poem's thesis but an
idea to which the poem responds dialectically. At the outset,
the title has no apparent relation to the poem at all:

> If there is a man white as marble
> Sits in a wood, in the greenest part,
> Brooding sounds of the images of death,
>
> So there is a man in black space
> Sits in nothing that we know,
> Brooding sounds of river noises;
>
> And these images, these reverberations,
> And others, make certain how being
> Includes death and the imagination.
>
> The marble man remains himself in space.
> The man in the black wood descends unchanged.

Rather than any direct statement about metaphor, we en-
counter a mystical and deeply mysterious scene. The two men
summoned as mythic presences are observed at a distance, as
sculpted images, yet the elements that compose them are largely
abstract. They have no clear symbolic meaning: the man white
as marble is associated with green (Stevens' usual symbol for
reality) and the man in black space exists in a realm beyond
the known world—suggesting that they represent reality and
imagination—but the former is preoccupied by synaesthetic
abstractions ("sounds of the images of death") while the latter
meditates on the more "realistic" (if strangely phrased) " sounds
of river noises." Although both images incorporate realistic
elements, both are essentially surreal. Most important is the
way in which they are linked, both through their parallel
attitudes and through the poem's syntax ("If there is . . . so
there is . . ."). Just as each man contemplates sounds anti-
thetical to the pole he seems to represent, so does the existence
of one of them immediately establish the existence of his
opposite. "Two things of opposite natures seem to depend /
On one another" (CP, 392): Being (or presence, or "reality")
must include death (or absence) and the imagination (or non-
"reality"), since by its very existence it defines them and thus
brings them into existence. This dissolving of polar opposi-
tion is enacted in the following lines: the two men, whose
static immobility is emphasized ("remains himself," "de-
scends unchanged"), in fact exchange places: the marble man,
formerly in the wood, is now "in space," while the man who
was in space now finds himself "in the black wood." Typi-
cally, the rhetoric of the poem does not emphasize this in-
terchange; readers must work against what the text seems to
say in order to discover its meaning.

The poem to this point has led us dramatically to the com-
plex experience of two ideas: that to define anything is to
establish the existence of its opposite, and that these opposites
share a fluid, mutually dependent relationship, rather than a
rigid polarity. Even if we have read the poem carefully and
imaginatively, we are forced here to make a surprising leap.

The focus shifts away from the men and toward the river that
to this point has been only overheard:

> It is certain that the river
>
> Is not Swatara. The swarthy water
> That flows round the earth and through the skies,
> Twisting among the universal spaces,
>
> Is not Swatara. It is being.
> That is the flock-flecked river, the water,
> The blown sheen—or is it air?

Swatara, a real river in Pennsylvania, is a detail that Stevens
uses a number of times in a characteristically playful way.
Here it ostensibly represents the single, particular river that
is distinguished from the immense, cosmic river of being. But
it is no accident that Stevens used Swatara instead of Delaware
or Potomac; he knew, as the echo of "swarthy water" makes
clear, that the word "Swatara" *sounds* dark, mysterious, ele-
mental. Again the apparent distinctions blur; we are told that
the river of being is unlike the real Swatara, yet it is impossible
to imagine what a river unlike a real river would be like. The
river overflows its channels, linking earth and "the universal
spaces," since it is both concrete particular ("the flock-flecked
river") and intangible abstraction ("or is it air?").

Thus we return to the idea expressed by the title. The
conception that metaphor is degeneration depends on the no-
tion that reality has an independent, primary existence, and
that imaginative projections of it are secondary, dependent,
and "unreal." Yet the experience of the poem strongly sug-
gests that being cannot exist—at least, cannot be experi-
enced—except through images of it, and that the real and the
imagined are joined in a mutually dependent flow:

> How, then, is metaphor degeneration,
> When Swatara becomes this undulant river
> And the river becomes the landless, waterless ocean?

Moreover, even when projected in its most surreal, metaphorical aspect, the river of being remains vital and undiminished. Since being includes death, the landless, waterless ocean can appear as the Styx without giving up any of its potency:

> Here the black violets grow down to its banks
> And the memorial mosses hang their green
> Upon it, as it flows ahead.

The vividly imagined deadly landscape is lush with vegetation; the green of the mosses is unexpected, and reminds us of the green, "real" wood of the first stanza. The more fully the ideas of the poem are embodied in images, the more keenly we experience them. Metaphor, in short, is not degenerative but regenerative. Only through the imaginative process can we approach the river of being, "the real made more acute by an unreal" (CP, 451).

An even more oblique treatment of the idea of metaphor is "Thinking of a Relation Between the Images of Metaphors" (CP, 356-57). Here the word "metaphor" is not mentioned except in the title, and the poem itself takes the form of a metaphysical parable:

> The wood-doves are singing along the Perkiomen.
> The bass lie deep, still afraid of the Indians.
>
> In the one ear of the fisherman, who is all
> One ear, the wood-doves are singing a single song.
>
> The bass keep looking ahead, upstream, in one
> Direction, shrinking from the spit and splash
>
> Of waterish spears. The fisherman is all
> One eye, in which the dove resembles the dove.
>
> There is one dove, one bass, one fisherman.
> Yet coo becomes rou-coo, rou-coo. How close
>
> To the unstated theme each variation comes . . .
> In that one ear it might strike perfectly:

State the disclosure. In that one eye the dove
Might spring to sight and yet remain a dove.

The fisherman might be the single man
In whose breast, the dove, alighting, would grow still.

The gently comic pastoral tableau explores the relation be-
tween perception and misperception. The bass fail to see that
the Indians and their waterish spears are long gone, but their
wary stillness is not out of place, since the fisherman poses
essentially the same deadly threat. In the same way, the fish-
erman fails to recognize the individual details of the landscape,
combining the wood-doves in his monocular and monaural
way into a single image—yet each dove retains its discrete
identity. The "reality" of the scene thus hovers between the
opposing principles of similarity, which reduces like elements
to a unified whole ("There is one dove, one bass"), and dif-
ference, which divides the unity into its separate components
("Yet coo become rou-coo, rou-coo"). This is precisely the
divergence in perspective suggested in the very early "Met-
aphors of a Magnifico" (CP, 19):

> Twenty men crossing a bridge,
> Into a village,
> Are twenty men crossing twenty bridges,
> Into twenty villages,
> Or one man
> Crossing a single bridge into a village.

As always in Stevens, the meaning of an image is determined
by—and floats between—those characteristics that identify it
as part of a particular class and those that make it unique. If
we apply this principle to the title of "Thinking of a Relation,"
the clear implication seems to be that while metaphor seeks
to bring images together in unified relation, the identities of
those images resist the reduction it necessarily requires.

The tone of the poem to this point is strikingly objective.
The focus widens to include not only the fisherman's view
of the doves, but also the reader's view of the fisherman ("one

fisherman"), yet each is described with equal detachment and precision. But in the sixth couplet the indicative mood gives way to the subjunctive, and what has been a straightforward description of present fact becomes a meditation on possibility. No matter "how close / To the unstated theme each variation comes," it remains a distinctively different entity—that is, unless the perceiving figure were transfigured as an ideal listener able to merge variation and theme, particular and general, into a single perception. Stevens suggests in 1947 in *The Necessary Angel* that "since, as between resemblances, one is always a little more nearly perfect than another and since, from this, it is easy for perfectionism of a sort to evolve, it is not too extravagant to think of resemblances and of the repetitions of resemblances as a source of the ideal. In short, metaphor has its aspect of the ideal" (NA, 81-82). But the ideal that departs from the particulars of experience is dangerously delusive. The fisherman is elevated to heroic stature only if his vision is capable of encompassing simultaneously both the specific, fully imagined dove and the general characteristics that unite it with other members of its species. Only then could the dove cease to oscillate between general and specific, between "coo" and "rou-coo," and grow still. Perhaps the image is meant to remind us of the dove sent out of Noah's ark. The resolution it represents suggests the tranquil moment described in "Notes toward a Supreme Fiction": "For a moment in the central of our being, / The vivid transparence that you bring is peace" (CP, 380). Stevens' skepticism prevents him from suggesting that this degree of unity can ever be achieved; it remains hypothetical, imaginary, a supreme fiction. But the poem does not end on a note of anxiety or desperation. The only way a unity between the disordered particulars of nature and the idealized patterns of imaginative vision can be realistically expressed is as open-ended possibility: "the relations between the ego and reality must be left largely on the margin" (NA, 79). The form of the poem, as well as its refusal to "state the disclosure" directly, leaves the reader to discover what must be the ideal "relation" toward which the images of metaphors move.

Stevens' most extended treatment of the idea of metaphor is "Someone Puts a Pineapple Together" (NA, 83-87), which appears as the second part of his 1947 essay, "Three Academic Pieces." The poem is clearly dramatic rather than transparent at the outset; one of its most stunning effects derives from its shift in the third section to the rhetoric of the transparent lyric. Assuming his familiar role of pedagogue, Stevens promptly complicates it by constructing the "lecture" on a narrative rather than a discursive frame: the pedagogue imparts not the fruit of his own experience, but that of a nameless "someone." Moreover, he demonstrates a strikingly fluid relationship to the "someone," observing him first at a distance, then gradually more intuitively and internally, until by the last section their two consciousnesses have merged. The poem is one of the best examples of Stevens' use of ideas, not as "truths" to be apprehended directly, but as themselves constituents of the dramatic texture. It is not so much a meditation as a poem about the experience of meditation, of developing interaction between the mind and the world.

The first section explores the paradoxical form of the pineapple, a natural object that looks so strangely surreal that it seems the imaginative transformation of something else:

> O juventes, O filii, he contemplates
> A wholly artificial nature, in which
> The profusion of metaphor has been increased.
>
> It is something on a table that he sees,
> The root of a form, as of this fruit, a fund,
> The angel at the center of this rind,
>
> This husk of Cuba, tufted emerald,
> Himself, may be, the irreducible X
> At the bottom of imagined artifice,
>
> Its inhabitant and elect expositor.

The tableau of man and pineapple we are asked to observe
seems as fixed a composition as the fruit itself. Yet if we look
carefully at the apparently static list of images with which the
pineapple is described, we see that in fact it shifts radically
from inner to outer, from Platonic form ("the angel at the
center of this rind") to solid object ("this husk of Cuba, tufted
emerald"). The movement from image to image forces us to
adopt the changing perspective of the participant, rather than
the summary view of the observer. If someone thinks he sees
"the irreducible X / At the bottom of imagined artifice," he
nevertheless continues to see the fruit itself. Moreover, the
irreducible X may simply be "himself." In attempting to take
the pineapple apart, to see through its metaphorical surface,
he may be peering into the equally "artifical" mirror of self-
consciousness. Both ways of looking at the pineapple, in other
words, necessarily involve the imagination: "the absence of
the imagination had / Itself to be imagined" (CP, 503).

> It is as if there were three planets: the sun,
> The moon and the imagination, or, say,
>
> Day, night and man and his endless effigies.
> If he sees an object on the table, much like
> A jar of the shoots of an infant country, green
>
> And bright, or like a venerable urn,
> Which, from the ash within it, fortifies
> A green that is the ash of what green is,
>
> He sees it in this tangent of himself.
> And in this tangent it becomes a thing
> Of weight, on which the weightless rests: from which
>
> The ephemeras of the tangent swarm, the chance
> Concourse of planetary originals,
> Yet, as it seems, of human residence.

Like the pineapple, any object on a table partakes of both pure
reality and pure imagination. But a third planet—the human
imagination—is required to link the other two in momentary

constellation. And since the imaginative configurations are constantly changing, the very nature of the object seen depends on the identity of the self that sees it. Given the endless possible permutations, the field of metaphor is enormous, but it is kept from mathematical expansion by its grounding in human invention.

To recognize that metaphor is a tangent of the self is to admit the threat of solipsism. If the contemplation of "someone" in the first section reveals that self is an integral component of metaphor, the second section explores the responsibilities thus inherent in that process. Again Stevens embodies his idea dramatically. In the first section, the pedagogue and the "someone" remain distinct, the former observing and commenting on the latter much as the latter in turn contemplates the pineapple. The conclusions about metaphor ("It is as if there were three planets") represent either the pedagogue's ideas or his intuition of the "someone's." But in the second section the subject-object distinction begins to break down, as a note of urgent conviction enters the poem:

> He must say nothing of the fruit that is
> Not true, nor think it, less. He must defy
> The metaphor that murders metaphor.
>
> He seeks as image a second of the self,
> Made subtle by truth's most jealous subtlety,
> Like the true light of the truest sun, the true
>
> Power in the waving of the wand of the moon,
> Whose shining is the intelligence of our sleep.

While the "someone" remains the central figure, he is no longer observed from a distance. The notion of responsibility expressed here is not a matter of intuition but of immediate self-knowledge. The "he," in short, shifts from an externalized to an internalized figure. And he recognizes that valid metaphor must adhere to reality—not to any narrow "prerogative jumble," but to the kind of truth shared equally by

truest sun and the power of fictive moonlight. The changes
of metaphor are more powerful—because more various and
subtle—than any purely natural metamorphosis:

> . . . The fruit so seen
> As a part of the nature that he contemplates
> Is fertile with more than changes of the light
>
> On the table or in the colors of the room.
> Its propagations are more erudite,
> Like precious scholia jotted down in the dark.

Like the definitions of "reality" and "metaphor," the ap-
proach to truth is twofold. The "forfeit scholar," with "his
enlargings and pale arrondissements," is unsatisfied by the
pineapple on the table, and seeks the "truth" that lies beyond
it. The "someone," on the other hand, searches for the ter-
ritory "where the truth was not the respect of one, / But
always of many things." Having left behind the world where
natural objects in themselves suffice, yet unwilling to abandon
them for the pale arrondissements of idealism, he seeks a place
where the transformations of metaphor are nevertheless true:

> . . . He had not to be told
>
> Of the incredible subjects of poetry.
> He was willing they should remain incredible,
> Because the incredible, also, has its truth,
>
> Its tuft of emerald that is real, for all
> Its invitation to false metaphor.
> The incredible gave him a purpose to believe.

In the final section of the poem, the truth of metaphor is
demonstrated overtly. The perspective shifts again: the ped-
agogue merges with the "someone," perceiving the pineapple
not indirectly but directly. Even his mask of pedagogue falls
away; his language becomes much richer and more sugges-

tive, and for the first time the voice speaks *from* rather than
about the moment of imaginative constellation:

> How thick this gobbet is with overlays,
> The double fruit of boisterous epicures,
> Like the same orange repeating on one tree
>
> A single self. Divest reality
> Of its propriety. Admit the shaft
> Of that third planet to the table and then:

The poem becomes at this point a transparent lyric. Losing
the distinction between subject (the pedagogue) and object
(the "someone," and beyond him, the pineapple), the reader
is drawn rhetorically into the action of the poem. The voice
generalizes to itself about the nature of imaginative vision
("When you divest reality of its propriety . . ."), but at the
same time it addresses to the reader a set of instructions about
how to see. The result of our assumed participation is im-
mediate; the pineapple appears in twelve metamorphoses, like
clockwork:

1. The hut stands by itself beneath the palms.
2. Out of their bottle the green genii come.
3. A vine has climbed the other side of the wall.

4. The sea is spouting upward out of rocks.
5. The symbol of feasts and of oblivion . . .
6. White sky, pink sun, trees on a distant peak.

7. These lozenges are nailed-up lattices.
8. The owl sits humped. It has a hundred eyes.
9. The coconut and cockerel in one.

10. This is how yesterday's volcano looks.
11. There is an island Palahude by name—
12. An uncivil shape like a gigantic haw.

The dazzling effect of this list depends on the ability of the
reader's mind to leap between the "planetary originals" and
the single object on the table. The meaning of the passage,

in other words, requires the reader to apprehend and recreate the "process of resemblance" on which it is structured.

The subsequent passage extends this principle farther, applying the process of metaphorical transformation to an idea rather than to an object. The idea—that since each metaphor is a "true" representation of the object, the object itself may be most nearly approximated by seeing it in as many different ways as possible—is itself developed through a series of strikingly imaginative metaphors. The parallelism might be emphasized by rearranging and numbering the lines as follows:

1. These casual exfoliations are of the tropic of
   resemblance.
2. Sprigs of Capricorn or as the sign demands.
3. Apposites, to the slightest edge, of the whole
   undescribed composition of the sugar-cone.

4. Shiftings of an inchoate crystal tableau.
5. The momentary footings of a climb up the pine-
   apple, a table Alp and yet an Alp.
6. A purple Southern mountain bisqued with the
   molten mixings of related things.

7. Cat's taste possibly or possibly Danish lore.

The relation of this last detail to the pineapple is mystifying, yet we are asked to affirm that, given the right perspective, the possible resemblance would be clear. Imagination is powerful enough to make any two objects near-relations: "the form, / At last, is the pineapple on the table or else / An object the sum of its complications, seen / And unseen. This is everybody's world." The truest reality, then, is composed of all possible metaphors of it.

Here the total artifice reveals itself

As the total reality. Therefore it is
One says even of the odor of this fruit,
That steeps the room, quickly, then not at all,

It is more than the odor of this core of earth
And water. It is that which is distilled
In the prolific ellipses that we know,

In the planes that tilt hard revelations on
The eye, a geometric glitter, tiltings
As of sections collecting toward the greenest cone.

When we recognize that the world cannot be perceived except
through the "prolific ellipses" of imaginative acts, then reality
and "the sum of its complications" become inextricably merged.
Thus even the scent of pineapple is not merely a physical fact
but a process of memory and imagination. Returning to the
fruit on the table, we cannot see it as a simple object. Putting
the pineapple together—which means both putting it together
with other objects in the act of metaphor and putting it *to-
gether*, giving it coherence and wholeness—has become a pro-
foundly creative act: "the world is no longer an extraneous
object, full of other extraneous objects, but an image" (NA,
151).

4

The Nothing That Is

> As if nothingness contained a métier,
> A vital assumption, an impermanence
> In its permanent cold . . .
>
> Stevens, "The Rock"

While Stevens wrote versions of the transparent lyric through-
out his career, his most sustained and original achievements
in the form occur among his late poems. The products of
Stevens' astonishing burst of creativity in his seventies have
often been unfavorably received; the poems in *The Auroras of
Autumn* were called by critics in the 1950s and early 1960s
variously "the utterances of an almost total inwardness,"[1]
"exercises in the exhaustion (trial by combat as it were) of
the urge to compose,"[2] "monumental wastes; transcendental,
all too transcendental, études; improvisations preserved for
us neither by good nor by bad, but by middle fortune."[3] In
recent years a number of excellent studies of the late poems
have appeared,[4] and the critical consensus now seems to value
them very highly. Yet it is worthwhile to examine some of
the claims on which negative criticism has been based, since
a number of these assumptions continue to impede our un-
derstanding of how these poems work and what they mean.

Negative judgments about the poems of *The Auroras of
Autumn* and *The Rock* have been based on curiously contra-
dictory grounds. On one hand, critics have argued that the
poems are distressingly impersonal and discursive, so far ab-

stracted from reality that they lack imaginative texture, and that they sacrifice creativity for the dreary articulation of ideas: "they are hardly the poems of a man who lives, loves, hates, creates, dies. Rather, they are the poems of a man who does nothing but make poems."⁵ On the other hand, it is often suggested that the poems are *too* personal, hermetically sealed from the reader by the inwardness of their references and movement, refusing to make the formal gestures we expect of lyric poetry:

> The critics' quarrel . . . is not simply against abstractness or creative fatigue. It is against the kind of thing Stevens would make poetry do, the audacity with which he would sit and muse, and publish those musings as poems because they came out iambic pentameter. . . . In a very special sense, they are poems over-committed: not to being poems, but to seeing how far the mind can go through language to apprehend a reality beyond language. . . . Are these poems not utterly solipsistic? . . . The answer would seem to be yes, that they are poems of a world (a mind) all its own.⁶

In light of these two claims, the poems sound both impossibly difficult and insufferably boring, like Schopenhauer in verse, or *The Waste Land* without objective correlatives. But the apparent contradiction between the charges of impersonality and solipsism suggests failure to examine carefully enough the nature of Stevens' achievement.

A frequent preoccupation of the late poems is the idea of aging and death. Many critics, apparently adopting Romantic notions of poetry as self-expression, take the frame of reference to be Stevens' own personal crisis of old age. For example, Helen Vendler writes, "These poems should tell us, if any can, of that undiscovered country of the old, and in fact they do, but it is a country rarely susceptible to language. When Stevens expresses the meaninglessness of his deprived days, the nameless weight of custom heavy as frost and deep almost as life, he cannot use the dramatic terms of his great

predecessors."[7] For Vendler, although Stevens' terms are dif-
ferent from those of his "predecessors"—her example is
Wordsworth—his motivation is essentially the same; she goes
on to read the poems as though they represented Stevens'
own spiritual autobiography. But if the references to aging
and death in the late poems are to be taken automatically as
expressions of the poet's own late anxiety—so that, for in-
stance, "An Ordinary Evening in New Haven" becomes "the
poem of an old man living in the lack and the blank"[8]—then
one wonders what to make of Vendler's description of "Like
Decorations in a Nigger Cemetery," written over fifteen years
earlier:

> The sense of death and fatal chill is the 'subject' of *Dec-*
> *orations*, as it will be the subject of *The Auroras of Autumn*,
> but to read only physical death into Stevens' lines is to
> limit his range. . . . Stevens is afraid, in his fifty-sixth
> year, that he is already shriveling into that dwarf form.
> His depletion is his specter, and his wrestlings with it
> make up *Decorations*.[9]

Vendler's tendency to attribute to Stevens submerged anxiety
and repressed desire surely betrays her here. For if death is
the subject of Stevens' early poems as well as his late work—
and it is a central preoccupation from *Harmonium* on—then
there is no justification for reading the late poems so exclu-
sively in terms of the poet's old age. While Merle Brown says
that "the ease of mind which dominates these poems . . . is
faithful to life, as Stevens's imagination has always been, but
the life to which it is faithful is the life of old age,"[10] I would
argue that this is to narrow severely the range of the poems.
Just as "death" in "Sunday Morning" refers not specifically
to the poet's own death but to the general fact of death, and
more broadly to the whole set of factors that delimit human
experience, so is the deliberate poverty of the late poems best
understood in its full metaphorical range.

This point is worth stressing for two reasons. To take the
primary subject of the late poems as "the intimate feelings of

the aged"[11] is ultimately to establish a barrier between the poet's experience and most readers', while if the form of the transparent lyric as I have defined it has any validity, the meaning of such poems depends on our ability to enter them as if their experience were ours. And second, the critics' insistence on reading the late poems in such narrowly autobiographical terms has I think obscured the design of the last phase of Stevens' work. By recognizing that the references to aging and death are part of a larger figurative pattern, we can see that they represent an extension or further exploration of, rather than a radical departure from, the preoccupations that were always central to Stevens' imagination. The late poems represent the relation between subject and object, "the difference that we make in what we see" (CP, 344), as a highly stylized antithesis: reality is seen as a condition of absence or blankness, which depends for its completion on the activity of imagination. At the same time, the late Stevens is never solipsistic. There is a crucial "meaning in nothingness" (CP, 438); as in "The Snow Man," "the nothing that is" there (CP, 9) is an integral part of the landscape. Rather than being evidence of personal anxiety, the references to death in the late poems serve to emphasize the universality of the ironic balance between presence and absence implicit in the act of consciousness.

One of the simplest examples of this balance is "The Woman in Sunshine" (CP, 445):

It is only that this warmth and movement are like
The warmth and movement of a woman.

It is not that there is any image in the air
Nor the beginning nor end of a form:

It is empty. But a woman in threadless gold
Burns us with brushings of her dress

And a dissociated abundance of being,
More definite for what she is—

Because she is disembodied,
Bearing the odors of the summer fields,

Confessing the taciturn and yet indifferent,
Invisibly clear, the only love.

Although the "content" of the poem is simply an extended
simile, the experience it provides is a deeply suggestive med-
itation on the act of imagination. As in Stevens' other trans-
parent lyrics, its meaning inheres in the shifts of apprehension
the reader is required to make. The title suggests the presence
of a woman in sunshine; the first four lines immediately deny
that presence. And once the two absolute poles of presence
and absence are established, the rest of the poem plays freely
in the territory between them. As the delicate ambiguity of
"the woman *in* sunshine" becomes apparent, its secondary
meaning—seeing sunshine *as* a woman—emphasizes Stevens'
fascination with the human tendency to anthropomorphize
by seeing metaphorically. The woman is emphatically both
there and not there; she is both physical (she "burns us with
brushings of her dress") and metaphysical (she also burns us
with "a dissociated abundance of being"). She is dressed in
gold (actual metal or pure color?), but the gold is threadless
(which does not resolve the ambiguity). Moreover, the states
of presence and absence exist not in uneasy opposition, but
in mutual dependence. The woman is "more definite," more
real, precisely because she springs "disembodied" out of empty
air.

   The poem to this point is concerned chiefly with establish-
ing the relations between the two poles, but in the final lines
the "reality" of the woman takes over, dissolving the dis-
tinction. Having accepted that the air is empty, we are forced
at the same time to acknowledge not simply a visual image,
but one highly charged with emotional overtones. As the
disembodied woman appears "bearing the odors of the sum-
mer fields," we recognize the same doubleness implicit in the
title. The invisible presence bears the odors, yet it is the odors
that evoke her presence in our imaginations. The emotion

with which she is invested is equally ambivalent and compelling: she comes to confess her love, but she is taciturn and indifferent. The poem moves toward suggesting the kinds of imaginative activity involved in any meaningful response to the natural world, but the allusive, mysterious language of the final couplet resists simple paraphrase—and thus forces the reader to engage in precisely that kind of imaginative response. Indeed, the poem's rhetoric is carefully controlled to draw us progressively into the experience. The first couplet sharply reverses our understanding of the title; by the middle of the poem we share the perception of the woman (she burns *us*); at the end we experience her as vital, enigmatic reality. The woman's love is "invisibly clear," which suggests both "transparent" and "apparent," and is thus an apt description of the woman herself, and of the imaginative act, spinning presence out of absence, that brings her to life.

The nothingness that nurtures vision and belief appears frequently in the late poems, but it is often more darkly colored than the empty summer air of "The Woman in Sunshine." The aurora borealis to which the title of "The Auroras of Autumn" refers is an image of magnificent beauty, but also of staggering power, which dwarfs the scale of human knowledge and experience. Confronting the terrifying sublime, the poet seeks to explain it in Canto VII by positing a destructive imagination, the dark double of creation, that snuffs out presences by a simple act of will:

> Is there an imagination that sits enthroned
> As grim as it is benevolent, the just
> And the unjust, which in the midst of summer stops
>
> To imagine winter? When the leaves are dead,
> Does it take its place in the north, and enfold itself,
> Goat-leaper, crystalled and luminous, sitting
>
> In highest night? And do these heavens adorn
> And proclaim it, the white creator of black, jetted
> By extinguishings, even of planets as may be,

Even of earth, even of sight, in snow,
Except as needed by way of majesty,
In the sky, as crown and diamond cabala?

Articulating the idea of malevolent imagination makes it true;
hypothetical questions give way to a statement of present,
violently inhuman action:

It leaps through us, through all our heavens leaps,
Extinguishing our planets, one by one,
Leaving, of where we were and looked, of where

We knew each other and of each other thought,
A shivering residue, chilled and foregone,
Except for that crown and mystical cabala.

No longer is this simply the poet's speculation. Characteris-
tically, the reader is implicated in the experience by the rhet-
oric that describes it. The emphatic first-person plural and the
brilliant conflation of tenses—so that the moment of destruc-
tion and the shocked recognition of the moment after are
collapsed into one—give the experience a chilling immediacy.
Yet the cosmic vacuum is as unstable as the presences it re-
placed; it must be fated to be overtaken in turn by a swing
toward the opposite pole:

But it dare not leap by chance in its own dark.
It must change from destiny to slight caprice
And thus its jetted tragedy, its stele

And shape and mournful making move to find
What must unmake it and, at last, what can,
Say, a flippant communication under the moon.
(CP, 417-18)

Harold Bloom calls this "the most surprising passage in *TAOA*,
and perhaps in all of Stevens." To Vendler's claim that Ste-
vens' transition here is an imposed order, not a discovered
one, he replies, "Stevens is neither imposing nor discovering
an order but rather uncovering a disorder, which is the de-

pendence of any hypostasis upon our wildness, our light ca-
price of freedom, if there is to be meaning of any kind."[12] A
simple affirmation of the human presence in the landscape
overturns the domination of absence; the magisterial power
of destruction is undermined by a casual gesture, a flippant
tone.

A number of poems represent the response to nothingness
as considerably more complex than the fatalistic knowledge
of its transience. One example is "In a Bad Time" (CP, 426-
27), which begins highly obliquely:

> How mad would he have to be to say, "He beheld
> An order and thereafter he belonged
> To it"? He beheld the order of the northern sky.

Since the northern sky is again cold and alien, beholding it
would presumably only increase our sense of distance from
it; the answer the question would seem to require thus is:
"Quite mad, indeed." But the poem immediately presents a
parable for our instruction:

> But the beggar gazes on calamity
> And thereafter he belongs to it, to bread
> Hard found, and water tasting of misery.
>
> For him cold's glacial beauty is his fate.
> Without understanding, he belongs to it
> And the night, and midnight, and after, where it is.
>
> What has he? What he has he has. But what?
> It is not a question of captious repartee.
> What has he that becomes his heart's strong core?
>
> He has his poverty and nothing more.
> His poverty becomes his heart's strong core—
> A forgetfulness of summer at the pole.

The beggar does not simply accept the winter vision, he lives
it. Rather than being alienated from the poverty in which he
lives, he becomes a part of it, turning himself into the snow

man. At the same time, he triumphs over nothingness by assimilating it, paradoxically making it a kind of presence on which he can draw for sustenance and strength. The tone here clearly implies a kind of heroism; the poem conducts a miniature dialogue with itself, forcing itself to give up "captious repartee" ("What has he? What he has he has.") for the more chastened and respectful "He has his poverty and nothing more." Still, the fact that the beggar belongs to calamity "without understanding," that he endures winter's cold only by forgetting about summer, suggests an ultimate reservation about his response. As the end of the poem implies, we are not all beggars, and some of us can be choosers. The final stanzas turn suddenly to a very different sort of figure:

> Sordid Melpomene, why strut bare boards,
> Without scenery or lights, in the theatre's bricks,
> Dressed high in heliotrope's inconstant hue,
>
> The muse of misery? Speak loftier lines.
> Cry out, "I am the purple muse." Make sure
> The audience beholds you, not your gown.

Again the line of thought is subtle, and the reader must bridge the gap unaided. Clearly, the beggar and Melpomene share parallel positions, her bare theater corresponding to his base poverty. But their responses differ. Rather than accepting and assimilating the condition of nothingness, Melpomene is exhorted to make herself into an emblem that will resist it. She is urged to "speak loftier lines," to learn that she is not "the muse of misery" but the muse of tragedy, to cultivate a style that will transcend her bare existence. This transformation cannot be simply cosmetic; Melpomene must become a great actress to accomplish her role. As in the final section of "Lapis Lazuli," the work of art represents a heroic act, the honest facing up to man's tragic condition that is paradoxically "joyous and jubilant and sure" (CP, 126).

     If "Puella Parvula" (CP, 456) does not represent the "loftier lines" of the tragic hero, it does suggest much the same response to a world seen as dissolving into blankness: the subduing of wild grief by the imagination, which shapes from it the powerful composure of art. The poem is one of the most exuberant and expressive of the whole body of Stevens' late work. The claim that it says "much the same thing as the earlier poetry, but with much less urgency and with an awareness that the saying and not the thing said is the life of the poem"[13] simply does not allow for the fact that its deliberately startling language and movement provide a reading experience altogether different from the earlier poems on the same "idea." To distinguish between "the saying" and "the thing said," particularly in such a dramatic poem, is to ignore the expressive function of "the saying," the degree to which in the transparent lyric meaning *consists* of immediate experience.

> Every thread of summer is at last unwoven.
> By one caterpillar is great Africa devoured
> And Gibraltar is dissolved like spit in the wind.
>
> But over the wind, over the legends of its roaring,
> The elephant on the roof and its elephantine blaring,
> The bloody lion in the yard at night or ready to spring
>
> From the clouds in the midst of trembling trees
> Making a great gnashing, over the water wallows
> Of a vacant sea declaiming with wide throat,
>
> Over all these the mighty imagination triumphs
> Like a trumpet and says, in this season of memory,
> When the leaves fall like things mournful of the past,
>
> Keep quiet in the heart, O wild bitch. O mind
> Gone wild, be what he tells you to be: *Puella*.
> Write *pax* across the window pane. And then
>
> Be still. The *summarium in excelsis* begins . . .
> Flame, sound, fury composed . . . Hear what he says,
> The dauntless master, as he starts the human tale.

Clearly, given key words like "unwoven," "devoured," "dis-
solved," "vacant," we are again in a landscape encroached on
by nothingness. But rather than the cold blankness of "The
Snow Man" or the shocked apprehension of section VII of
"The Auroras of Autumn," here the tone has a distinctly
comic edge. The threat of oblivion is offset in the first stanza
by the disparity between "great Africa" and Gibraltar on the
one hand and the science-fictional devouring caterpillar and
the colloquial "spit in the wind" on the other. The great
impact of Stevens' "nothingness" is felt when it is internalized
as spiritual desolation; here, externalized and exaggerated, it
feels considerably less ominous.

The next two stanzas continue this ironic distancing. To
express the immanence of destruction, the poem adopts the
image of a vast, roaring wind. But the metaphors that describe
the wind are so lively and inventive that the impression the
lines make is not essentially destructive but creative and ex-
pansive. The extended sentence, with its clauses strung out
in apposition and its emphatic gerunds and participles ("roar-
ing," "blaring," "trembling," "gnashing," "declaiming"),
becomes a celebration of variety and multiplicity. The real
wind is immediately transformed into its own "legends." The
savage beasts of Armageddon are deflated: the elephant is
perched on the roof like a cartoon figure, and since the lion
is *either* in the yard *or* about to spring from the clouds, it loses
any pretense to bloody realism. When, in the fourth stanza,
we are told that "over all these the mighty imagination
triumphs," it is only to describe what we have already seen
in practice: the movement toward destruction has indeed been
transfigured by the imagination.

The long sentence comes to an end in a startling way. The
direct address of "O wild bitch. O mind / Gone wild" seems
designed to bring us up short, and the metaphoric distance
between tenor and vehicle is dissolved. Since there is no ob-
vious figure for the poem to be addressing, and since our
hearts and minds have presumably been excited by the imag-
inative action of the first half of the poem, we might guess

that *we* are being addressed. But if the imagination is deeply involved in the description of the chaos, how is it suddenly detached from and opposed to it? Who is the "he" who is suddenly in command of the mind? *"Puella"* reminds us of the title, but how can the "very little girl" be the same as the wild bitch? In fact a wonderfully mysterious dissociation has taken place. The imagination is both acting in the poem and controlling its movement from outside, the reader is both involved participant and detached observer, the mind *is* both wild bitch and little girl in turn. Then, through a powerful tonal resolution, both confusion and despair are calmed; the prominent use of Latin, and the command to "write *pax* across the window pane," suggest that language is the key to controlling the chaos and to achieving a resolution of the self. The sound and fury of inhuman destruction are composed by the imagination into "the human tale" that begins as the poem ends. Humanized and pacified even in the face of winter's approach, the mind is ready to turn from nature's chaotic noise and listen to the heroic tale of art. And of course in reading the poem that is precisely what we have done.

In "Study of Images II" (CP, 464–65), the balance between absence and presence is evoked by a meditation on the ontology of images, and specifically their double status as both rooted in reality and detached from it. The texture of the poem is dense and mysterious; it is animated by tension between the carefully objective perspective suggested by the title and the lively surrealism of the images themselves. The clash between the rational and irrational elements of the poem mirrors the disjunction between reality and imagination that is Stevens' central concern, and extends to the poem's language, syntax, and movement. The reading experience that results is both complex and rewarding, and repays close attention.

>The frequency of images of the moon
>Is more or less.

The first line echoes the dry precision of the title, promising a straightforward declarative statement, but the end of the sentence thwarts this expectation, distorting normal grammar

(The frequency is more or less?) and producing a nonsense statement (more or less than what?). As in "Puella Parvula," language itself is partly the subject, but here, rather than being the key to order, language seems inadequate to the poem's slippery concerns.

> The pearly women that drop
> From heaven and float in air, like animals

> Of ether, exceed the excelling witches, whence
> They came.

The wonderfully evocative pearly women are presumably examples of images of the moon, but beyond that general impression it is difficult to follow what is being said about them. It is not clear in what way the women exceed the witches, or why they come from them—though the movement of the poem suggests that the witches are something like ur-images of the women, and that the women exceed them in being better (that is, more faithful, more evocative) images of the moon. The poem continues to combine static, rather elevated diction ("exceed," "whence") with dreamlike, almost nonsensical patterns of thought.

> But, brown, the ice-bear sleeping in
>   ice-month
> In his cave, remains dismissed without a dream, . . .

The "but" establishes a contrast that allows the underlying logic of the poem to begin to emerge: on the one hand, fluid, exceedingly excellent images, and on the other, an isolated dormant figure. The bear is so far removed that he seems almost to have disappeared into the landscape, to have become an "ice-bear sleeping in ice-month"—which also seems to distance him temporally, into the archaic compound formulas of medieval poetry. "Without a dream" might mean that the bear is not dreaming, but it is more likely that the bear is dismissed because no one is dreaming of him, and this is borne out by the next stanza:

> As if the centre of images had its
> Congenial mannequins, alert to please,
> Beings of other beings manifold—

This is a brilliant conceit: *Spiritus Mundi* as a department store, full of images willing to be posed and dressed at the imagination's whim, and dependent on "other beings" for their own life. Images are stockpiled in a kind of limbo until the imagination makes them living presences. The relative clarity of the idea suggests confidence that images have now been "placed" and understood. But the "as if" makes the idea tentative, and the next stanza complicates the issue considerably:

> The shadowless moon wholly composed of shade,
> Women with other lives in their live hair,
> Rose—women as half-fishes of salt shine, . . .

These powerful images seem to rise of their own accord, each formed of bright figure and its dark opposite: a fusion of the new moon and the full, the medusa, the mermaid. The apparition of these images at this point in the poem, taking over as center of attention, suggests a measure of autonomy beyond the role of "congenial mannequins." Moreover, since the images appear to stand syntactically in apposition to the previous stanza, the implication is that the "other beings" of which images are manifold are not simply those who imagine them, but also their dark doubles in the limbo of nothingness. Presences depend for definition on absences: the shadowless moon is wholly composed of shade. Appropriately, the syntax here is tangled—it is unclear whether the moon or the women (or both) rose, or why the dash comes in the middle of the third line rather than at the end—but the confused complexity of the thought is demonstrated perfectly. And out of this tangle breaks the ending:

> As if, as if, as if the disparate halves
> Of things were waiting in a bethrothal known
> To none, awaiting espousal to the sound

> Of right joining, a music of ideas, the burning
> And breeding and bearing birth of harmony,
> The final relation, the marriage of the rest.

Again "as if" is emphasized, but its repetition, rather than
multiplying the tentative status of the idea, suggests instead
the excitement of discovery. From the frustrating attempt to
separate image from idea, as indicated by the knotty language
and rhythm of the previous stanzas, springs the realization
that they are inextricably related in the act of imagination.
The understanding seems instinctive rather than intellectual:
the language tumbles over itself in its haste to reach a con-
clusion. Presence and absence, images and their negative dou-
bles, are mutually dependent, but they exist in a mysterious,
static "bethrothal" (the archaic form continues the "literary"
quality of the poem's vision) until they are animated by the
imagination, the "music of ideas." Thus released into fruitful
marriage, they produce a satisfying harmony. "The final re-
lation" must remain hypothetical, but it can be imagined.

"Study of Images II" is an interesting poem in itself, but
it is even more significant as an introduction to "An Ordinary
Evening in New Haven" (CP, 465-89), which it immediately
precedes in *The Auroras of Autumn*. "Study" demonstrates
Stevens' deep interest in the dynamic relation of consciousness
to blankness, presented rather mystically as the tension be-
tween images "present" because they are realized and those
"absent" because they are not. This problem is also the center
of the meditation composing "An Ordinary Evening." To
say that the poem focuses on "a depression which is over-
whelmingly physical—the metabolic depletion in age of the
body's resources"[14] seems reductive. "Reality" in Stevens' last
long poem is not simply the poverty of old age but the noth-
ingness against which every consciousness, young or old,
must continually assert itself. The poem is extremely complex
and too long for full examination here. But since its structure
is that of variations on a theme, and since Stevens himself
first published an abbreviated version, we may without much

damage examine separate sections, to study Stevens' treat-
ment of the idea.

The movement of "An Ordinary Evening," like that of
Stevens' work in general, is double. In some sections the mind
presses outward, toward unmediated confrontation with the
bare poverty of experience: "the poem of pure reality, un-
touched / By trope or deviation" (CP, 471). Other sections
move toward recognizing the essential power of imagination,
which mediates and transforms the nothingness that sur-
rounds it. Section IV is one of the latter, as its first line sug-
gests:

> The plainness of plain things is savagery,
> As: the last plainness of a man who has fought
> Against illusion and was, in a great grinding
>
> Of growling teeth, and falls at night, snuffed out
> By the obese opiates of sleep.

"Plain things" are of course the components of reality un-
varnished by imagination, and the sense of the first line seems
clearly to be that such things are too real to be comfortably
endured. But the parabolic scene that purports to illustrate
this idea proves, characteristically, to be more complication
than illustration: the rhetoric forces us to revise our expec-
tations. The man who fights against illusion struggles toward
the immediate apprehension of reality; he would presumably
reach it in death, the ultimate reality that destroys all links to
the past. This is what the poem's extravagantly dramatic lan-
guage leads us to believe happened ("the last plainness . . . a
great grinding / Of growling teeth, and falls at night, snuffed
out"). But his "last plainness" turns out to be plain irony: his
quest for bare reality is defeated by the least savage enemy,
sleep. Stevens' comic gift is apparent here: the grinding,
growling teeth belong not to some hideous beast but to the
man himself, and the agents of sleep are transfigured as fat
assassins. The last plainness is that we cannot pursue plainness
too long; the grace of imagination invariably descends:

> Plain men in plain towns
> Are not precise about the appeasement they need.
>
> They only know a savage assuagement cries
> With a savage voice; and in that cry they hear
> Themselves transposed, muted and comforted
>
> In a savage and subtle and simple harmony,
> A matching and mating of surprised accords,
> A responding to a diviner opposite.

Plainness and imagination and the harmony that occasionally results from their union are all equally savage, which in this context means both fierce and uncontrolled. That harmony is also unpredictable; imaginative integration is made to seem a natural process, and the seasonal cycle is again invoked:

> So lewd spring comes from winter's chastity.
> So, after summer, in the autumn air,
> Comes the cold volume of forgotten ghosts,
>
> But soothingly, with pleasant instruments,
> So that this cold, a children's tale of ice,
> Seems like a sheen of heat romanticized.

As in "Puella Parvula," autumn is the season of memory. The mists that rise both resemble the figures of ghosts and serve as ghostly reminders of summer's shimmering heat. This ethereal vision of the past is far from painful; hot reality is metamorphosed into pastoral romance, like the Snow Queen's palace in the fairy tale. Yet the "subtle and simple harmony" with which the section ends is also savage, since to accept the romanticized tale of winter would be to court disaster. The bare reality of cold inevitably returns, and imagination's soothing assuagement gives way to the last plainness of death.

Although the oscillation between the poles of presence and absence is a constant of our experience, that experience never fails to be surprising and mysterious. Given the richness of imagination, Stevens suggests in section X, the seasons of belief are no more mechanical than the natural seasons:

It is fatal in the moon and empty there.
But, here, allons. The enigmatical
Beauty of each beautiful enigma

Becomes amassed in a total double-thing.
We do not know what is real and what is not.

The moon's fated, predictable change becomes a kind of fa-
tality, which the mystery of our experience enables us to
avoid. The real and our perception of it are finally inseparable;
"reality" includes "not merely the visible, / The solid, but
the movable, the moment" (CP, 471-72), and this compli-
cation is what divides our spiritual fluctuation from what
Stevens elsewhere calls "planetary pass-pass" (CP, 425).

We say of the moon, it is haunted by the man

Of bronze whose mind was made up and who,
      therefore, died.
We are not men of bronze and we are not dead.
His spirit is imprisoned in constant change.

But ours is not imprisoned.

To this point, the language of section X is conversationally
flat ("a total double-thing," "We are not men of bronze and
are not dead"), the rhythm unemphatic and choppy ("But,
here, allons," "who, therefore, died"). But when the freedom
of the human spirit is described, the poem becomes more
transparent and achieves exuberant lyricism:

It resides
In a permanence composed of impermanence,
In a faithfulness as against the lunar light,

So that morning and evening are like promises kept,
So that the approaching sun and its arrival,
Its evening feast and the following festival,

This faithfulness of reality, this mode,
This tendance and venerable holding-in
Make gay the hallucinations in surfaces.

While lunar light is simply a physical principle, our changeable perspective casts everything we experience in terms of human values. Thus the rising and setting of the sun seem not merely astronomical facts but signals of the faithfulness of the universe, and sunrise and sunset seem ritual celebrations. Celebrating human values in the landscape is precisely the opposite perspective from that of "The Snow Man," and what we know about Stevens should prepare us to expect a qualification. It comes in the final line, which, although still affirmative, is a rather tentative conclusion to the section. "Gay" is a delicate description of the pyrotechnical festival of sunset, or of our response to it. The passage leads us to desire a stronger affirmation, but the rhetoric, like the facts of our existence, resists it. In fact, the "venerable holding-in" which allows us to color our reality with human values may be simply the suppression of a larger awareness. The final words of the section embody this awareness; even as the human perspective is being celebrated, the poem forces the recognition that "this mode" of seeing depends finally on "hallucinations in surfaces." Again we are subtly urged to turn back to bare reality itself.

As section XXII indicates, the turn to reality is itself problematical—not only is the real tightly bound to our imaginative perception of it, the nature of the quest itself is unclear:

> Professor Eucalyptus said, "The search
> For reality is as momentous as
> The search for god." It is the philosopher's search
>
> For an interior made exterior
> And the poet's search for the same exterior made
> Interior: breathless things broodingly abreath
>
> With the inhalations of original cold
> And of original earliness.

The philosopher and the poet pursue the same pure reality in entirely different ways. The philosopher seeks the central truth on which all exterior reality depends, the common root of all

experience, while the poet searches for the objective fact that
corresponds to his own subjective knowledge. Despite their
differences, each conceives of reality as an unknown that can
be reached only by going beyond or beneath the known, and
both see the search for reality as a breathless quest beyond
presences for the cold absence that preceded them.

> Yet the sense
> Of cold and earliness is a daily sense,
>
> Not the predicate of bright origin.
> Creation is not renewed by images
> Of lone wanderers. To re-create, to use
>
> The cold and earliness and bright origin
> Is to search.

Without denying Professor Eucalyptus's claim for the im-
portance of the search for reality, the poem suggests that the
quest must be defined in a different way. Reality lies, not
beyond presences, but in them; the cold and earliness that
symbolize "the nothing that is" are not remote unknowns
but daily experiences. Moreover, it is wrong to think of reality
as the province only of intrepid explorers ("lone wanderers"),
since the daily recreation of the self and confrontation with
experience is itself a search for what is real.

The passage thus far is dry, abstract, and difficult, and
reading it is largely a matter of puzzling out the rather abstruse
language. But having presented an idea in the style of Pro-
fessor Eucalyptus, Stevens caps it with one that is concrete
and playful:

> Likewise to say of the evening star,
> The most ancient star in the most ancient sky,
>
> That it is wholly an inner light, that it shines
> From the sleepy bosom of the real, re-creates,
> Searches a possible for its possibleness.

Masking ("Likewise") as a continuation of the quest for bare
reality, the statement is actually directed toward the imagi-

nation. The evening star is presumably thoroughly external, immeasurably distanced from us in time and space. To suggest that it is in fact internal, and to locate it in "the sleepy bosom of the real" (a wonderfully physical reversal of the remote, chilly "reality" of the earlier stanzas), seems merely an act of fancy. Yet since the statement reorders the facts of our existence and thus creates a new order, examining a possibility for the possibility that it is true, it is also part of the search for reality. Stevens stops far short of asserting that acts of imagination constitute our chief means of approaching reality; the delicate, tentative last stanza forces us to draw our own conclusions.

Section XXVIII begins with the supposition that the real exists only as we conceive of it, and brings it graphically to life by casting reality as a nun ("misericordia" is the clue) in her mental convent cell:

> If it should be true that reality exists
> In the mind: the tin plate, the loaf of bread on it,
> The long-bladed knife, the little to drink and her
>
> Misericordia, it follows that
> Real and unreal are two in one: New Haven
> Before and after one arrives or, say,
>
> Bergamo on a postcard, Rome after dark,
> Sweden described, Salzburg with shaded eyes
> Or Paris in conversation at a café.

The ideas by this time are familiar, yet their realization—the evocative convent properties, the list of impressions of cities—continues to be inventive and convincing. A city imagined in anticipation and then actually experienced remains essentially the same, even if the details differ, since in each case it is perceived from the confines of one's own vision. New Haven after one arrives is not "real" New Haven, but one's own version of it, just as a postcard can only provide one view of the city it pictures.

The passage then turns abruptly inward, and remarks about itself:

This endlessly elaborating poem
Displays the theory of poetry,
As the life of poetry. A more severe,

More harassing master would extemporize
Subtler, more urgent proof that the theory
Of poetry is the theory of life,

As it is, in the intricate evasions of as,
In things seen and unseen, created from nothingness,
The heavens, the hells, the worlds, the longed-for lands.

Helen Vendler uses this passage to demonstrate that "An Or-
dinary Evening" represents a decline from the earlier long
poems, "as even Stevens himself seems to have recognized
when he called it 'this endlessly elaborating poem' and wished
that it could have been written by 'a more severe, more har-
assing master' who could propose 'subtler, more urgent proof'
than he could himself."[15] This view results from her tendency
to see the late poems primarily as expressive of Stevens' own
self-conscious anxiety. I would claim that there is nothing
self-deprecating here: to call "An Ordinary Evening" "end-
lessly elaborating" is not a confession of failure but a simple
statement of the consequences of choosing to write a series
of poems that seek to draw the reader into an endlessly elab-
orating subject. To draw a neat, succinct conclusion would
be to falsify the complex impression Stevens means to convey.
He risks the "imitative fallacy," but in large part he succeeds
convincingly. Besides, the statement is slyly ironic, since the
poem is in fact not endless but only three sections from its
conclusion. Stevens does not wish that the manner of the
poem were different, that he (or anyone else) could assemble
"subtler, more urgent proof." It is perfectly apparent in read-
ing the poem that "the theory / Of poetry is the theory of
life," that the imagination is essential to all varieties of per-
ception. But because Stevens is not a didactic poet, he does
not harass us into his perspective. Rather, he adopts the tactics

of the transparent lyric, offering us not "proof" but the imag-
inative experience of ideas.

In section XXX we return to the stripped silence of late
autumn, the last moment before the total blankness of winter.
The landscape is described with precise equanimity:

> The last leaf that is going to fall has fallen.
> The robins are là-bas, the squirrels, in tree-caves,
> Huddle together in the knowledge of squirrels.
>
> The wind has blown the silence of summer away.
> It buzzes beyond the horizon or in the ground:
> In mud under ponds, where the sky used to be
>   reflected.

Life is almost entirely deprived of "the intricate evasions of
as"; the one metaphor ("tree-caves") is frankly primitive. Here
Stevens seems to have achieved completely his aim "to get
as close to the ordinary, the commonplace and the ugly as it
is possible for a poet to get. It is not a question of grim reality
but of plain reality. The object is of course to purge oneself
of anything false" (L, 636). The buzzing wind seems vaguely
ominous, yet Stevens refuses to sentimentalize or personify
the scene. Emptiness is not to be viewed as loss, but as a
reduction to essentials, a search for reality enacted by natural
processes:

> The barrenness that appears is an exposing.
> It is not part of what is absent, a halt
> For farewells, a sad hanging on for remembrances.
>
> It is a coming on and a coming forth.
> The pines that were fans and fragrances emerge,
> Staked solidly in a gusty grappling with rocks.

Fragrances and inventive perspectives disappear, leaving only
solid physical forces like trees and rocks. In such a limited
field of objects, even the air gains potency and value; the
transparent medium is itself an integral part of reality:

The glass of the air becomes an element—
It was something imagined that has been washed away.
A clearness has returned. It stands restored.

It is not an empty clearness, a bottomless sight.
It is a visibility of thought,
In which hundreds of eyes, in one mind, see at once.

The cumulative movement of "An Ordinary Evening" brings
us to this moment of dazzling vision. For a moment at the
edge of winter the eye and the mind are unified, and the pure
reality we perceive is not emptiness but clarity. The object of
the vision is carefully unspecified, since reality is not in the
object but in the process by which it is perceived. Ideally, as
readers we have been brought by the medium of the trans-
parent lyric to exactly this perspective; we have achieved "a
visibility of thought," a unity of image and idea, through
which reality is perceived with heightened clarity and under-
standing.

5

Machines Made of Words

Always, in a work of art, leave a large part to the imagination
of the spectator, thus to arouse his imagination also (never
block it) & give him work to do. For that is the prime des-
tination of the thing produced, the created object, the new
born infant, to have the beholder through his imagination *take
part* in it, thus & only thus to complete it.

Williams, notebook entry dated 10/18/50

To link Stevens with William Carlos Williams in a discussion
of poetic genre may seem to some readers rather quixotic.
The two are popularly presented as antithetical in intention
and vision: Stevens as persistently subjective, repeatedly flirt-
ing with solipsism in his obsession with acts of the mind,
Williams as the stubbornly objective poet of "no ideas but in
things." Each regularly appears as counterpoint in critical dis-
cussions of the other. Thus Hugh Kenner, for example, says
that Stevens' "Thirteen Ways of Looking at a Blackbird"
"coheres by postulating a maximal separation between what
is said and what is experienced. . . . This assumption is the
polar opposite of Williams' assumption that words share
thinghood with things, and that language is a social fact need-
ing no explanations. A Williams poem becomes as unintel-
ligible, if we make a puzzle of how words relate to reality,
as a Stevens poem does if we do not."[1] Joseph Riddel also
argues that their assumptions about language are fundamen-
tally opposed:

The essential difference is this: language for Williams must be made to work upon the world, bringing that world to form while preserving its diversity even within the perceiver; language for Stevens is the form into which the incessant exchanges of self and world flow, the syntax of inwardness or fiction. It does not describe the world, much less effect changes in the world; it describes the world in the mind.[2]

Denis Donoghue states this difference most firmly: Williams "had no interest in the kind of thing that interested Stevens: philosophy, ontology, epistemology, gorgeous nonsense of the mind. . . . If he saw a blackbird, he had no interest in the thirteen ways in which Stevens saw it: one way was enough, given reasonable lucidity. This is to say that Williams was a moralist, not a philosophic poet."[3]

In previous chapters I have attempted to demonstrate that Stevens' posture toward experience is considerably more complex and less inward than many accounts suggest. In turning to Williams, I hope to refute the similarly one-sided notion that his poems attempt simply to transcribe the world objectively. Williams is primarily interested not in the physical world in itself, but in the dynamic relationship between the world and the life of the mind as it apprehends and responds to that world. To differentiate Stevens from Williams, Riddel describes him as follows:

Stevens' images are, essentially, metaphors of consciousness, or states of consciousness. They are the products of a perception, but a perception refreshed; moreover, they exist not in static arrangements (fixed perceptions) but in a state of process or flow, describing the landscape of a sensibility rather than the landscape of a physical world. Stevens' images adhere to a world of things . . . with striking fidelity, but only in the sense that they catch the moment in which mind and thing marry.[4]

I would claim that exactly the same relationship is found in Williams' poems, and that although his techniques are quite different, many of his most original poems embody a delicate balance of mind and thing in the form of the transparent lyric.

Uncertainty about the relationship between the work of the two poets perhaps reflects to some degree the ambivalent personal relationship between them. In the foreword to his autobiography, Williams expresses surprise that Stevens is "scarcely mentioned, though he is constantly in my thoughts" (A, xii), but in light of other evidence this seems less than surprising. Though they met in 1914 and kept in touch periodically throughout the rest of their lives, they appear to have made each other uneasy. In 1922, Stevens writes to Harriet Monroe, "Williams drove through town a few weeks ago on his way to Vermont with one of his children and a dog. It was a blessing to see him although we were both as nervous as two belles in new dresses" (L, 228). In a 1948 letter he calls Williams "a man somehow disturbed at the core and making all sorts of gestures and using all sorts of figures to conceal it from himself" (L, 592). Williams caricatures Stevens in his 1920 prologue to *Kora in Hell*:

> Wallace Stevens is a fine gentleman whom Cannell likened to a Pennsylvania Dutchman who has suddenly become aware of his habits and taken to "society" in self-defense. He is always immaculately dressed. I don't know why I should always associate him in my mind with an imaginary image I have of Ford Madox Ford. (I, 15)

Though both poets felt impelled to stay on the periphery of the New York literary world rather than leap into the mainstream, and demonstrated strikingly parallel needs to balance their work in poetry with the more practical careers of law and medicine, their temperamental differences kept their relationship cordial rather than close.

This personal tension is carried over into their critical judgments. In 1935 Stevens writes that Marianne Moore's work

seems considerably more important than Williams': "I cannot
help feeling that Williams represents a somewhat exhausted
phase of the romantic, and that his great attractiveness is due
to the purity of his form" (L, 278-79). He seems to have felt
threatened by Williams' technical experiments; he writes in
1946, "I have the greatest respect for him, although there is
the constant difficulty that he is more interested in the way
of saying things than in what he has to say" (L, 544), and in
1953 pursues the idea: "I am not too sure that my own way
of thinking of things is right, particularly when I come across
the universal acceptance of Bill Williams, for instance, who
rejects the idea that meaning has the slightest value and de-
scribes a poem as a structure of little blocks" (L, 803). Wil-
liams' displeasure with the introduction Stevens wrote for his
Collected Poems 1921-1931 (in which Stevens calls Williams a
romantic poet) is well-documented, and although he never
grouped Stevens in the enemy expatriate camp of Eliot and
Pound, he clearly lamented his failure to join his own search
for a native idiom: "Stevens is a troubled man who sings well,
somewhat covertly, somewhat overfussily at times, a little
stiffly but well. If he were satisfied with that! . . . Five beats
to the line here, and that's where the trouble is let in. These
five beats have a strange effect on a modern poet; they make
him think he wants to think. Stevens is no exception. The
result is turdigity, dullness and a language, God knows what
it is! certainly nothing anybody alive today could ever rec-
ognize."[5] Even Williams' memorial tribute to Stevens is cu-
riously ambivalent:

> He was a man who would never acquire the stigma of
> a popular appeal. He never stepped down to that. There-
> fore he earned an undeserved reputation for coldness if
> not sterility. . . . Contemplation, vividly casting its lights
> across his imagination, sufficed for him. . . . It colored
> all he wrote with flashes from an imagination—as if he
> was speaking from under water—that the sun pierces

with a slightly out of focus light. When he became a realist it was never in his own person.[6]

Given Williams' avowed passion for realism and immediate contact with experience, his portrait of Stevens as aloof and masked suggests a poet with whom he felt he had little fundamentally in common.

Nevertheless, beyond their obvious differences in temperament, Stevens and Williams shared basic assumptions about experience, language, the imagination, and the crucial role of poetry in twentieth-century America. Whatever Stevens' reservations about the forms Williams' poems took, he always valued him as "one of the few people in this country that really has an active and constant interest in writing" (L, 768). *Spring and All* (1923) defends and celebrates the imagination in terms often strikingly similar to those of *The Necessary Angel* (1951). Stevens sounds much like Williams when he comments on the native character of American poetry ("Nothing could be more inappropriate to American literature than its English source since the Americans are not British in sensibility" [OP, 176]) or his own response to reality ("My principal concern . . . is not so much with the ideas as with the poetry of the thing" [L, 289]). And a passage in Williams' 1940 play, *Many Loves*, echoes "Of Modern Poetry" to a remarkable degree:

No one knows what poetry
should be today. It should be the
audience itself, come out of itself
and standing in its own eyes, leaning
within the opening of its own ears,
hearing itself breathe, seeing itself
in the action—lifted by poetry to
a world it never knew, a world it has
always longed for and may enter for a
few precious moments never to be known
in prose. The audience is the play.
And it is pure poetry—unless one

fails to imagine it and lift it beyond
the dirty boards into the empyrean.
                                        (ML, 33)

I have used "Of Modern Poetry" to explore the role Stevens
constructs for his readers in the transparent lyric; this passage
corresponds so closely that it invites similar exploration. In
this chapter I intend to show that, however different his poems
were from Stevens' in form and voice, in fact throughout his
career Williams developed his own version of the transparent
lyric, which has the same aesthetic and philosophical signif-
icance as Stevens'.

One characteristic of the transparent lyric—its conception
not as the record of an achieved experience but as an exercise
in the process of vision—is a notion more common in criticism
of Williams than of Stevens. Williams has, on the whole, been
better served by criticism, partly because his overtly experi-
mental techniques have forced attention to the nature of the
reading experience to a degree that Stevens' more subtly in-
novative style has not. Williams' own theoretical writings also
emphasize the spontaneity and immediacy fundamental to his
notion of modern art. In calling the poem "a field of action,"
in constructing poems in such a way as to underscore the acts
of attention inherent in reading them, in calling art "some-
thing comparable to nature: an other nature" (SE, 303), he
draws attention to the focus on active process characteristic
of the transparent lyric. In his 1939 essay, "Against the
Weather," he argues for "the salutary mutation in the expres-
sion of all truths, the continual change without which no
symbol remains permanent. It must change, it must reappear
in another form. . . . What is a man saying of moment as an
artist when he neglects his major opportunity, to build his
living, complex day into the body of his poem?" (SE, 208,
217).

As Paul Mariani's recent biography makes clear, Williams
was a man of deeply romantic temperament, and growing up
as he did with the impassioned subjectivism of Keats and

Whitman as his dominant influence, it is not surprising to find him speaking as if the poet's own experience were central in his conception of art. Early in his career he describes his ambition as completely subjective: "I must write, I must strive to express myself. I must study my technique, as a Puritan did his Bible, because I cannot get at my emotions in any other way. There is nothing save the emotions: I must write, I must talk when I can. It is my defiance; my love song: all of it."[7] In 1927 he suggests that the artist focuses inward, producing art simply for his own well-being: "To vary between knowing and feeling is the artist's purgatory, living in which he keeps alive by losing his life, in a brutal sense, and losing it by making 'plays,' objects, realities which he has to abandon to make another, and another—perfectly blank to him as soon as they are completed" (SE, 56). And as if to mirror these attitudes, much of the criticism, like that of Stevens, treats Williams' poems as if they were grounded in an expressive theory of art. Roy Harvey Pearce, for example, calls "The Red Wheelbarrow" ("so much depends . . .") "notably sentimental," and then continues:

> Williams can only dimly specify "what" depends—himself in his vocation as poet. He assures himself that he is what he is by virtue of his power to collocate such objects into sharply annotated images like these. He must feel himself into the things of his world; for he is as dependent on them as occasions to be himself—as poet. Perhaps—and herein lies the pathos—they depend on him as much as he depends on them.[8]

Rod Townley defines the "implicit" posture of the early poems as that of advice: "The advice of the poems in *Spring and All* is to open one's sensibilities to the world, and when the world presents one (as it will) with some unexpected and unexplainable perfection, to record only those details that *most* strike one."[9] I would argue that Williams is anything but indifferent to his readers, and that the poems in *Spring and All* are constructed neither as exercises in self-assurance nor as advice

about how to write poems. But determining exactly what
relationship they establish between the reader, the poet, and
the world entails considerable difficulties.

These difficulties are compounded by Williams' tendency
to refer to "the imagination" and "the poem" as independent
entities, as in such passages in *Spring and All* as this:

> Imagination is not to avoid reality, nor is it description
> nor an evocation of objects or situations, it is to say that
> poetry does not tamper with the world but moves it—
> It affirms reality most powerfully and therefore, since
> reality needs no personal support but exists free from
> human action, as proven by science in the indestructi-
> bility of matter and of force, it creates a new object, a
> play, a dance which is not a mirror up to nature but—
> As birds' wings beat the solid air without which none
> could fly so words freed by the imagination affirm reality
> by their flight. (I, 149-50)

Williams' criticism, almost always deeply metaphorical, is
here so oblique as to be of little use in teaching us how to
read the poems. Presumably by "the imagination" here he
refers to his own, which in the act of writing poems liberates
words and allows them to "dance over the body of his con-
dition accurately accompanying it" (I, 149). But earlier in
Spring and All he says, "In the imagination, we are from
henceforth (so long as you read) locked in a fraternal embrace,
the classic caress of author and reader. We are one. Whenever
I say 'I' I mean also, 'you.' And so, together, as one, we shall
begin" (I, 89). On this passage Hillis Miller comments, "Wil-
liams' readers must abandon their separate selves and lose
themselves in the imagination of the poet, sharing with him
there in the action whereby every man, woman, and child on
the face of the earth is annihilated."[10] Miller thus turns the
focus back on the poet's imagination and makes it primary.
But I would argue that, rather than requiring self-abnegation,
Williams' statement does just the opposite, insisting that the
reader share equally, fraternally, in the experience of the poem.

Surely the way in which Williams' discussion of "the imag-
ination" tends to blur the distinction between poet and reader
is suggestive of the relationship he intends to establish. Al-
though Miller envisions readers being subsumed into the
monistic world of Williams' imagination, the quotation seems
more accurately to establish a dialectic, joining reader and
poet "together, *as* one," each maintaining independent integ-
rity. This is the double vision of the transparent lyric, and
Williams' description of the way in which it is accomplished
is strikingly similar to the method I have attributed to Stevens:
"The attempt is being made to separate things of the imagi-
nation from life, and obviously, by using the forms common
to experience so as not to frighten the onlooker away but to
invite him" (I, 107). By presenting the imaginative vision in
forms common to the reader's experience—rather than forms
restricted to the subjective experience of the poet or a dram-
atized speaker—the transparent lyric seeks to draw the reader
in, to allow him to experience that vision directly, while still
retaining his own "separate self."

    A second persistent source of confusion is the question of
Williams' "impersonality." One reason for this confusion is
Williams' own criticism: he never seems to sense the possible
contradiction between his insistence that the artist express
reality through the liberating medium of his own imagination,
and his definition of the poem as "a small (or large) machine
made of words" (SE, 256). A few years after the highly per-
sonal, idiosyncratic performance of *Spring and All*, he iden-
tifies as the source of great art the ability to lose one's per-
sonality in one's subject: "Shakespeare had that mean ability
to fuse himself with everyone which nobodies have, to be
anything at any time, fluid, a nameless fellow whom nobody
noticed—much, and *that* is what made him the great dram-
atist" (I, 253). And after writing poems as dogmatic as "Tract"
and "To a Solitary Disciple," he says in a 1934 letter, "All
I'm interested in—or almost all—is impersonally, as imper-
sonally as possible, to get the meaning over and see it flourish"
(SL, 151). Williams' insistence on the term "impersonal," and

his machine metaphor, have led some critics to assume that he means to disengage the poem from subjective experience altogether.[11] This seems to me a fundamental misconception. The poems are not self-denying, since sometimes explicitly ("so much depends"; "I must tell you") and always implicitly—through the details of their composition and arrangement—they are evidence of an imaginative self confronting the world. As Neil Myers says, "The artist as active, subjective, personal presence does not dominate the book, but the *creating* artist certainly does. . . . *Spring and All* may be impersonal, but it is not dehumanized; it is simply neither romantic nor expressionistic."[12] The machine metaphor thus speaks not to the vision the poem communicates but to the way in which it communicates it: the poet always brings subjective experience to the act of writing, but once the poem is complete it must stand independent of that experience, as much a created object as a machine, "an other nature."

Poetry for Williams thus should be both subjective and impersonal simultaneously. Ironically, Williams' use of the word "impersonality" is strikingly similar to what Stevens meant in his introduction to Williams' *Collected Poems 1934* by "anti-poetic," the term to which Williams violently objected. Williams assumed that Stevens intended to divide experience into two camps, the poetic and the anti-poetic, a distinction with which he could obviously not agree. As the context makes clear, Stevens actually refers to two ways of looking at experience, and by "anti-poetic" simply means the attitude opposed to what is stereotypically thought poetic, the sentimental: "The anti-poetic is his spirit's cure. He needs it as a naked man needs shelter or as an animal needs salt. To a man with a sentimental side the anti-poetic is that truth, that reality to which all of us are forever fleeing" (OP, 255). Stevens was one of the first to recognize that Williams' poetry is born from the dialectic of opposites, and that it seeks to balance subjective experience with objective forms:

> Something of the unreal is necessary to fecundate the
> real; something of the sentimental is necessary to fe-

cundate the anti-poetic. Williams, by nature, is more of
a realist than is commonly true in the case of a poet.
. . . The essential poetry is the result of the conjunction
of the unreal and the real, the sentimental and the anti-
poetic, the constant interaction of two opposites. This
seems to define Williams and his poetry. (OP, 256)

It is only one further step to recognize that one way to achieve
this doubleness was to focus on the experience evoked in the
poem rather than on an individual experiencing it. "The only
human value of anything, writing included, is intense vision
of the facts" (I, 259), Williams writes in 1927, having already
begun to evolve his version of the transparent lyric to evoke
the facts as immediately as possible for his reader.

Once we understand how Williams uses "impersonality,"
it becomes clear that the reading experience is not incidental
to his concept of poetry, that, in fact, it is central. In *Kora in
Hell* (1920) Williams writes,

> The thing that stands eternally in the way of really good
> writing is always one: the virtual impossibility of lifting
> to the imagination those things which lie under the direct
> scrutiny of the senses, close to the nose. It is this dif-
> ficulty that sets a value upon all works of art and makes
> them a necessity, (I, 14)

and nineteen years later he is still saying it: the real purpose
of poetry is "to lift the world of the senses to the level of the
imagination and so give it new currency" (SE, 213). Williams'
characteristically oblique reference to "the imagination" can-
not conceal that he refers here to a communicative value:
poetry is necessary because it lifts reality to the *reader's* imag-
ination. It is precisely to accomplish this vividly and accurately
that impersonality is necessary, as Williams' emphasis on the
antithesis between saying and making affirms:

> When a man makes a poem, makes it, mind you, he
> takes words as he finds them interrelated about him and
> composes them—without distortion which would mar
> their exact significances—into an intense expression of

his perceptions and ardors that they may constitute a
revelation in the speech that he uses. It isn't what he
says that counts as a work of art, it's what he makes,
with such intensity of perception that it lives with an
intrinsic movement of its own to verify its authenticity.
(SE, 257)

This statement is extremely revealing of the paradoxical dual-
ity of Williams' conception of poetry: the poem as "intense
expression of his perceptions and ardors," and the poem as
independent, "made" object. Powerful subjectivity is clearly
a necessary part of the creative moment, and the work of art
is intended to produce an equally subjective response in the
reader ("to lift the world of the senses to the level of the
imagination"), but the agent of communication is the "in-
trinsic movement," the authenticity of the poetic medium.
"It is in the minutiae—in the minute organization of the words
and their relationships in a composition that the seriousness
and value of a work of writing exist—*not* in the sentiments,
ideas, schemes portrayed" (SE, 109). The poem thus becomes
not the secondary record of an event but the primary event
itself, not symbolism, "not 'realism' but reality itself— . . .
not a matter of 'representation' . . . but of separate existence"
(I, 117). And in an unpublished essay Williams extends this
notion specifically to include its effect on the reader: "nothing
'about' the subject, a bare placing of the matter before the
attention, as an object, that which with wit a man might see
for himself—swiftly and to the point."[13]

Critics have emphasized the way in which Williams' use of
metaphor serves to join—momentarily and often inade-
quately—various elements of the world into coherent wholes.[14]
Williams' universe, as he remarks repeatedly throughout his
career, is tragically fragmented, alienated, "divorced," and
the aim of poetry—by which he means not simply words on
the page but any act of imagination—is "through metaphor
to reconcile / the people and the stones" (CLP, 7). Both his
sense of the correspondence that might be achieved between

the self and nature, and his determination to achieve it through the medium of imagination, reveal his Romantic heritage. "The great creations, like those of the past in every case, arise from the close ties between the poet and the upsurging (or down surging) forms of his immediate world,"[15] he writes in 1946. Suzanne Juhasz sees Williams' use of metaphor as an outgrowth of this correspondence:

> Metaphor functions in Williams's poetry as the linguistic embodiment of the imagination. The imagination, for Williams, is that power which mediates between the mind and the world. It liberates both words and objects by transposing them into the medium of the imagination. Williams uses metaphor to define the relations that exist between the particular forms and objects in the world. He views these relations in terms of dualities, so that metaphor's primary function is to suggest the nature of dualities and, especially, to conjoin their elements.[16]

This description is suggestive but incomplete in that it focuses entirely on the action of the *poet's* imagination. Williams is distinguished from his Romantic forebears in the way in which his poems bring the imagination into play. Metaphor, linguistically defined, is, in fact, far less common in the poems than imaginative resemblance which is *implied* by association and juxtaposition. Imagination is for Williams much less important as a way of asserting his own vision than as a way of making the world real enough for the reader to experience it freshly and spontaneously: "the value of the imagination to the writer consists in its ability to make words. Its unique power is to give created forms reality, actual existence" (I, 120). The poem is thus not an expression of metaphoric unity; rather, it presents reality in such a way as to allow the reader to experience unity first-hand.

In fact, I would claim that for Williams the poem itself functions metaphorically, joining the reader into the movement which the poem enacts. In 1943 he criticized Louis Zukofsky for a style that made "jerky, hysterical reading" be-

cause it was "too broken, too unexplicit to bridge the gap
between the writer and the reader,"[17] thus charging the poem
itself with a metaphorical function he elsewhere attributes to
the imagination. Poems are similarly intended to bridge the
gap between the reader and the world, drawing the reader
into an immediate experience analogous to that of the world
at large:

> There is a constant barrier between the reader and his
> consciousness of immediate contact with the world. . . .
> The reader knows himself as he was twenty years ago
> and he has also in mind a version of what he would be,
> some day. Oh, some day! But the thing he never knows
> and never dares to know is what he is at the exact mo-
> ment that he is. And this moment is the only thing in
> which I am at all interested. (I, 88, 89)

And in a passage in *Kora in Hell* Williams makes explicit the
degree to which this relation departs from the Romantic model:
"That which is heard from the lips of those to whom we are
talking in our day's-affairs mingles with what we see in the
streets and everywhere about us as it mingles also with our
imaginations. . . . Nowadays the elements of that language
are set down as heard and the imagination of the listener and
of the poet are left free to mingle in the dance" (I, 59). The
image suggests a spontaneous street-dance, reflecting natural
freedom as well as aesthetic form, rather than a carefully chor-
eographed performance. The poem becomes an active field
of living language, in which the reader, rather than watching
the poet perform on a stage, is equally free to "mingle in the
dance." This is, of course, a fanciful image, and it remains to
be seen how such freedom is to be achieved in practice.

A crucial aspect of Williams' attempt to join the reader and
the poem, as of Stevens', was to use the poem to present
facets of experience brokenly, without completing or closing
them. As life does not deliver itself in neatly coherent and
ordered packages, neither should the poem. The meaning of

the poem thus depends fundamentally on the reader's ability
to confront and respond to it:

> Always, in a work of art, leave a large part to the imag-
> ination of the spectator, thus to arouse his imagination
> also (never block it) & give him work to do. For that
> is the prime destination of the thing produced, the cre-
> ated object, the new born infant, to have the beholder
> through his imagination *take part* in it, thus & only thus
> to complete it.[18]

In another passage Williams even suggests that the words of
the poem may be seen as accompaniment to the reader's un-
derstanding, which represents the poem's true content:

> The inexplicitness of modern verse as compared with,
> let us say, the *Iliad*, and our increasingly difficult music
> in the verse as compared with the more or less down-
> rightness of their line forms—have been the result of a
> clearly understandable revolution in poetic attitude.
> Whereas formerly the music which accompanied the
> words amplified, certified and released them, today the
> words we write, failing a patent music, have become
> the music itself, and the understanding of the individual
> (presumed) is now that which used to be the words.
> (SL, 125-26)

At the same time, Williams is of course conscious that this
freedom is in an important sense illusory, and that the reader's
response is in fact carefully controlled by the poet. The poem
is not a do-it-yourself kit, and neither its order nor its meaning
is left to chance. In writing of George Antheil's music that
the listener's "alert mind . . . goes any way it can from point
to point, brokenly if it must" (SE, 59), Williams is perfectly
aware that, provided the listener is paying attention, the
movement has been conditioned by the composer. And his
early comment on Joyce is explicit:

In the work of James Joyce the underlying fact which has impressed me is that by the form of his thought he has forced the reader into a new and special frame of mind favorable to the receipt of his disclosure. By his manner of putting down the words it is discovered that he is following some unapparent sequence quite apart from the usual syntactical one. That is of course the power behind all good writing. (SE, 28)

In my first chapter I suggested that developments in the painting and sculpture of the early part of the century helped Stevens and Williams develop transparence as a rhetorical mode; these comments demonstrate that modern music and fiction were also important influences.

Williams' attempt to invite the reader's imagination into participation in the dance extends beyond the kind of experience the poems present, to the formal patterns in which they present it. He is deeply sensitive to the kinetic quality of poetry—"as in all machines its movement is intrinsic, undulant, a physical more than a literary character" (SE, 256)—and for Williams this movement becomes an essential element of the poem's meaning, since it controls the way in which the reader apprehends the experience. This helps explain Williams' lifelong preoccupation with metrics; often his nearly metaphysical rationales for the variable foot, the native rhythm, the triadic line make him appear a mystic of technique, but actually his technical experiments and innovations serve primarily to order the field of attention, to structure in straightforward ways the acts of the mind that compose the poem. Williams' use of syntax and lineation to control emphasis, to vary pace, and to modulate revelation is extraordinarily intricate and supple—as I intend to demonstrate—and has figured prominently in criticism. Thomas Whitaker, for example, focuses on the demands Williams makes on the reader's attentiveness:

The mind itself must listen. It must attend to the forward impetus, hesitations, changes of direction, conflicting motions, ambiguities, sudden shocks, and resolutions that inhere in the controlled placement of syntactical units. This timed release of meaning is essential to Williams' verse. . . . His own full "measure," which he was never able to describe adequately, inheres in the mental and kinesthetic response to the texture of sequential units of attention.[19]

Yet the idea that the field of the reader's attention is crucial to the meaning of the poem is not always so clearly recognized. Elsewhere Whitaker says of the poems, "When successful, they are themselves dramatic structures of attentive or contactful speech; and that achievement is their primary meaning."[20] To speak of poems as composed of "attentive or contactful speech" implies the centrality of a speaker, and suggests that the reader's role is that of a listener rather than an active agent. While this is an apt description of such poems as "This Is Just to Say" and "The Last Words of My English Grandmother," it fails to account adequately for those poems that in one way or another are deliberately *not* mimetic of natural dramatic speech. Many of Williams' most characteristic poems pulse with the fragmented, literally inarticulate rhythms of a mind in action—sketching, redoubling, revising an idea—or even of the less than fully conscious registration of perceptions, rather than the linear progression of attentive speech. The reader of such poems is forced by their formal patterns to enact these rhythms in order to understand them, since he or she cannot perceive them as a particular person's experience. The movement, in short, *is* the experience, and thus—in Williams' eyes—is inseparable from the meaning of the poem.

One other aspect of the poems' movement needs clarification. It is common to speak, as Whitaker does in the passage just quoted, of Williams' use of the line as a unit of attention.

That this is true in only a particular sense should be clear from
"Between Walls" (CEP, 343):

BETWEEN WALLS

the back wings
of the

hospital where
nothing

will grow lie
cinders

in which shine
the broken

pieces of a green
bottle

Obviously, broken phrases like "of the" and "will grow lie"
are not units of attention in terms either of normal syntax or
of natural cognition or perception; they are units of attention
only for the reader engaged in reading the poem. Hillis Miller
interprets this technique as having deeply metaphysical sig-
nificance:

A pregnant tension is given to words and the spaces
around them by ending a line in the middle of a phrase.
. . . Going for the moment toward the void, they go
all the more strongly, as a man in isolation reaches out
in longing toward other men and women. Into the white
space surrounding the word go a multitude of lines of
force, charging that space with the almost tangible pres-
ence of the various words which might come to com-
plete the central word and appease its tension.[21]

But it seems to me useful to follow the lead of Williams'
discussion of other writers' distortions of language, and to
see the abrupt lineation primarily in terms of its immediate
effect on the reader. About Gertrude Stein, for example, he

emphasizes the element of surprise: "The goal is to keep a
beleaguered line of understanding which has movement from
breaking down and becoming a hole into which we sink dec-
oratively to rest" (SE, 118). And he praises the way in which
Marianne Moore uses words to achieve "rapidity of move-
ment. A poem such as 'Marriage' is an anthology of transit.
It is a pleasure that can be held firm only by moving rapidly
from one thing to the next. It gives the impression of a passage
through" (SE, 123).

Variety is one of Williams' touchstones. Each of his vol-
umes after the very earliest exhibits a wide range of attitudes,
voices, and forms, and beyond a rather facile limit it is difficult
to identify systematic development in his work. There is no
point in his career—as I believe there is in Stevens'—at which
the transparent lyric becomes his predominant and most char-
acteristic form. Many of his poems of course exist primarily
to exhibit the genuine poetry inherent in the rhythms of speech,
and may be properly classified as variants of the dramatic
monologue or dramatic lyric. Yet to read through Williams'
collected poems is to realize how often he was drawn to write
poems without a particularized speaker, without a voice in
any dramatic sense. By tracing the development of the trans-
parent lyric in Williams' career, I hope to illuminate both the
way in which the form evolved for him and the particular
uses and variants he invented for it.

The poems of *Poems* (1909) and *The Tempers* (1913) are
mannered and highly dramatic. Written variously in imitation
of what Williams took to be the Keatsian sublime, and later
of Pound, they are deeply subjective and romantic lyrics, and
their syntax is characteristically exclamatory: "The archer is
wake! / The Swan is flying!"; "And thou, beloved, art that
godly thing!"; "Take that, damn you; and that!" Those few
not written in the first person still manifest an intensely per-
sonal emotion or perspective: "Mighty shall he be / Red cra-
dle of the night, / The dusky child!!" In accordance with
Pound's 1913 principles of Imagism, the language and rhythms
of *Al Que Quiere!* (1917) are considerably more natural and

relaxed; almost all the poems still employ or suggest an opaque speaker. One exception is "Winter Quiet" (CEP, 141):

> Limb to limb, mouth to mouth
> with the bleached grass
> silver mist lies upon the back yards
> among the outhouses.
>   The dwarf trees
> pirouette awkwardly to it—
> whirling around on one toe;
> the big tree smiles and glances
>   upward!
> Tense with suppressed excitement
> the fences watch where the ground
> has humped an aching shoulder for
>   the ecstasy.

Yet although the poem has no clearly dramatized speaker, it remains entirely subjective; its motivation is expressive, to project a fanciful vision of the landscape in winter. The extravagant metaphors (erotic mist, excited fences) and personification (trees pirouetting and smiling, the ground's ecstatic aching shoulder) reveal much more about the idiosyncratic poet than about the landscape itself. And the reader's role is still to witness this rapturous self-projection and to be convinced (or not convinced, as the case may be) of its authenticity. Another poem expressing an immediate response to nature is "Dawn" (CEP, 138):

> Ecstatic bird songs pound
> the hollow vastness of the sky
> with metallic clinkings—
> beating color up into it
> at a far edge,   —beating it, beating it
> with rising, triumphant ardor,—
> stirring it into warmth,
> quickening in it a spreading change,—
> bursting wildly against it as

dividing the horizon, a heavy sun
lifts himself—is lifted—
bit by bit above the edge
of things,—runs free at last
out into the open—! lumbering
glorified in full release upward—
songs cease.

Again there is no characterized "I," but the poem manifests
the judgment and vision of a particular ego. "Dawn" is more
successful than "Winter Quiet" in evoking the activity of a
natural scene, largely through its insistent participles and
breathless movement, yet we still view it through the eyes of
a persona who sees nature as expressive of mood: bird songs
as ecstatic, the night sky as hollow, the sun as male and strug-
gling to escape into freedom, and so on. In both poems, the
exclamation points suggest an unwillingness to let the details
speak for themselves, or an uncertainty that they can convey
the emotional charge the poet intends them to have. As James
Breslin says of the volume as a whole, Williams "is too con-
spicuously present as teacher, artist, and personality."[22]

By the time of *Sour Grapes* (1921), Williams has learned to
replace exhortation with a subtler description, and to begin
to involve the reader in a more direct and imaginative way.
"The Lonely Street" (CEP, 227) is a good example:

School is over. It is too hot
to walk at ease. At ease
in light frocks they walk the streets
to while the time away.
They have grown tall. They hold
pink flames in their right hands.
In white from head to foot,
with sidelong, idle look—
in yellow, floating stuff,
black sash and stockings—
touching their avid mouths
with pink sugar on a stick—

like a carnation each holds in her hand—
they mount the lonely street.

The most obvious difference from the earlier poems is tone:
precise, declarative statements have replaced melodramatic
exclamations and sentimental metaphors. The poem gains en-
ergy and complexity by playing off this restrained tone against
the subjectivity that inheres in its localized perspective. Care-
ful reading reveals a shifting, uncertain perception of the
schoolgirls, implying a point of view to be identified with a
particular observer. Almost immediately the poem contradicts
itself, moving from "It is too hot / to walk at ease" to "At
ease / in light frocks they walk the streets." The girls are first
perceived as dressed "in white from head to foot," then "in
yellow, floating stuff, / black sash and stockings." The candy
they are eating shifts from "pink flames in their right hands"
to "pink sugar on a stick" to "like a carnation each holds in
her hand," each phrase carrying significantly different con-
notations. The protean quality of the description may reflect
the changing angle from which the observer views the girls
as they pass along the street, or his playful imagination; in
any case, it manifests the subjectivism in which the poem is
grounded, and which makes it essentially dramatic. What brings
the poem closer to the transparent lyric is the way in which
this subjectivism is modulated, even hidden, by the tone.
Only the reader who sees beyond the even tranquillity can
perceive the double perspective, which in turn supports the
tension between innocence and inherent eroticism at the the-
matic center of the poem.

Another poem from the same volume is "Blizzard" (CEP,
198):

Snow:
years of anger following
hours that float idly down—
the blizzard
drifts its weight
deeper and deeper for three days

or sixty years, eh? Then
the sun! a clutter of
yellow and blue flakes—
Hairy looking trees stand out
in long alleys
over a wild solitude.
The man turns and there—
his solitary tracks stretched out
upon the world.

Again a double perspective is achieved, here not by juxta-
posing subjective perceptions with an objective tone, but by
working on several different associative levels simultaneously.
The rhetoric implies a dramatic speaker who seeks approval
("eh?") and exclaims his observation of "the sun!" But while
"Blizzard" is, like "Winter Quiet," the expression of a sub-
jective view of the landscape, it does not proceed with the
same sort of openly assertive statements; "Winter Quiet" sim-
ply projects its personified vision outward, but "Blizzard"
turns inward, implying its view of the scene through subtle
indirection. The colon at the end of the first line signals a
metaphorical identity between the snow and the complex ab-
straction that follows, but the poem makes no overt attempt
to trace out or make more explicit the relation between the
heaviness of the mounting snow and the weight of accumu-
lated anger. The reader of "Winter Quiet" is expected simply
to assent to the metaphorical vision, while reading "Blizzard"
effectively requires making judgments about its associations
and implications, about the relation between the objective and
the subjective statements it makes. The link between the nat-
ural scene and the private weather is deeply felt, though the
specific details and circumstances are not revealed. Is the sun's
appearance simply a naturalistic detail, or does it have sym-
bolic significance, given what precedes it? Why is flat, entirely
objective description ("Hairy looking trees") deliberately jux-
taposed against subjective vision (the landscape as "a wild
solitude")? Is the man of the final sentence a separate figure

seen symbolically in the snow, or is he the persona himself,
suddenly objectified and distanced? Since I read the poem as
centering on the tension between the self and the world, the
associations that emerge between subjective and objective ways
of seeing, I do not believe any of these questions can be de-
finitively answered, or is meant to be. The inner and outer
worlds blur in the act of reading the poem, as they do for the
persona. At any rate, the fact that the question of interpre-
tation arises is one measure of the emerging role of the reader
in determining the meaning of the poems.

In some of his poems of the 1920s, Williams succeeds in
further submerging the dramatic role of the speaker, avoiding
assertive statements of judgment or insight, while at the same
time building on structures of tension or dialectical process
in order to avoid the static quality he believed by this time
to be the failure of imagism. The subject of *Spring and All*
(1923) is the dynamic energy of the imagination, and the
structure of the volume as a whole, darting erratically between
poetry and prose, serves to transfer that energy to the reading
experience. Individual poems also formally evoke the same
kind of activity. One of the most familiar, "By the road to
the contagious hospital" (CEP, 241-42), may be seen as tran-
sitional between the dramatic lyric and the transparent lyric.
Its structure reflects the dynamic tension between a static,
almost photographic description of the landscape and an in-
tuition of the organic energies of growth inherent in the land-
scape—which is in turn mimetic of the conflict in the volume
between winter and spring, or the conflict in Williams' poetics
between prose and poetry. The beginning of the poem, aside
from the ubiquitous circumstances of selection and arrange-
ment, is almost entirely free of evidence of Williams' "pres-
ence" as a poet:

> By the road to the contagious hospital
> under the surge of the blue
> mottled clouds driven from the
> northeast—a cold wind. Beyond, the

waste of broad, muddy fields
brown with dried weeds, standing and fallen

patches of standing water
the scattering of tall trees

All along the road the reddish
purplish, forked, upstanding, twiggy
stuff of bushes and small trees
with dead, brown leaves under them
leafless vines—

We recognize, of course, Williams' careful use of sound, lin-
eation, and repetition ("standing . . . standing . . . upstand-
ing") to control the way we apprehend this world; but the
world itself we seem to experience directly, through its own
colors, textures, and shapes, rather than through any extrav-
agantly subjective metaphors the poet might impose on it.
That the blue clouds "surge" instead of "rush" or "billow,"
and that the muddy fields compose a "waste," does imply a
measure of judgment, but certainly the predominant impres-
sion is of impersonal observation. As the focus shifts from
present circumstances to immanence and possibility, though,
the poem moves through sympathetic projection *into* the land-
scape:

Lifeless in appearance, sluggish
dazed spring approaches—

They enter the new world naked,
cold, uncertain of all
save that they enter. All about them
the cold, familiar wind—

As the new, vital organisms are personified, the central con-
sciousness of the poem itself comes into view, reflecting, in
Stevens' terms, not a mind of winter but the tendency to see
natural forms in human terms. In the final stanzas, the two
modes of the poem alternate, moving from the knowing an-
ticipation of "Now the grass, tomorrow / the stiff curl of

wildcarrot leaf" to the nearly scientific precision of "One by
one objects are defined— / It quickens: clarity, outline of leaf,"
and then back to humanized description:

> But now the stark dignity of
> entrance—Still, the profound change
> has come upon them: rooted, they
> grip down and begin to awaken

Roy Harvey Pearce says of the poem, "A perception of a
series of objects is made to blend into a thought ('It quick-
ens:'), so that it *is* the thought."[23] I believe rather that the two
kinds of apprehension are juxtaposed but *not* blended, and
that the tension between them is a crucial aspect of the reading
experience.

Another *Spring and All* poem, "The Sea" (CEP, 275-76),
achieves an equally effective tension in an entirely different
way, through placing evocative and yet highly cryptic images
in striking juxtaposition. The poem proceeds by a series of
declarative statements, but the magisterial source of those
statements cannot be identified dramatically; the reader thus
confronts a powerful set of perceptions without a clear way
to link them, and the reading experience is not unlike plunging
into a deep and changeable ocean. The simultaneous flow of
visual, auditory, and tactile imagery is overpowering, so that
paraphrasable content is often submerged beneath a purely
sensual surface. Its musical qualities are hypnotic; in fact, at
several points the language turns into pure sound ("ula lu la
lu," "coom barroom"), as if the sheer vitality of the sea's
sound (which the poem imitates throughout) were resisting
the attempt to shape it into human speech.

Beneath the restless and highly kinetic surface, the poem
reflects a complicated response to the sea. Rather than "an
intellectual and emotional complex in an instant of time," it
builds a deeply ambiguous image from constantly shifting
perspectives, suggesting first alternately and then simultane-
ously both eroticism and deathliness.

The sea that encloses her young body
ula lu la lu
is the sea of many arms—

The blazing secrecy of noon is undone
and and and
the broken sand is the sound of love—
The flesh is firm that turns in the sea
O la la
the sea that is cold with dead men's tears—

Deeply the wooing that penetrated
to the edge of the sea
returns in the plash of the waves—

a wink over the shoulder
large as the ocean—
with wave following wave to the edge

coom barroom—

The opening stanzas suggest a narrative center, but the scene cannot be fixed into a stable time, space, or point of view; for instance, it seems to take place both during the day ("the blazing secrecy of noon") and at night ("the night is deep," we are told later). The young woman who is intermittently the focus seems to be alone, yet it is hard to reconcile this with the repeated images of lovemaking ("the sound of love," "the wooing that penetrated / to the edge of the sea"). "The sea that encloses her body / . . . is the sea of many arms," suggesting both a Hindu erotic god and the deadly embrace of an octopus. "The flesh is firm that turns in the sea"; the firmness and the turning are seductive, yet the coldness of the line ("the flesh" rather than "her body") makes explicit the possibility—implicit from the first line—that the poem is describing a drowned corpse drifting in the surf. To seize on this as the "clue" to the poem would be to violate its delicate subtleties; "The Sea" is not a detective story to be solved by the reader, but a way of stimulating us to imaginative vision.

Through all the ambiguous evocation we hear the changing
song of the sea, whose wordlessness and indifference empha-
size the essential mystery at the center of the poem. James
Breslin identifies this kind of utterance with the beautiful and
destructive lure of the sirens,[24] surely a key association, yet
again it does not "solve" the poem. This is also the sea itself
speaking, emphasizing that for Williams the world's vitality
and mystery (and the poem that reproduces them) constantly
resist the constraints of artistic form and critical knowledge.
The tension of perspectives builds:

> It is the cold of the sea
> broken upon the sand by the force
> of the moon—
>
> In the sea the young flesh playing
> floats with the cries of far off men
> who rise in the sea
>
> with green arms
> to homage again the fields over there
> where the night is deep—
>
> la lu la lu
> but lips too few
> assume the new—marruu
>
> Underneath the sea where it is dark
> there is no edge
> so two—

"The young flesh playing" is juxtaposed against the cries of
the men with green arms. By this point the poem has acquired
a parodic quality: the men with green arms are presumably
the waves themselves, grotesquely anthropomorphized in a
mockery of the conventionally literary sea-poem. At the same
time they also suggest drowned men, wreathed in seaweed,
rising in an ominous yet genuinely mythic act of homage to
the land. The ending of the poem confirms and blends these
poles of meaning without resolving them. In the penultimate

stanza the poem turns back on itself, almost dissolving again into pure sound (the rhymes are so insistent as to sound grating and banal), yet retaining inferences of erotic connection. And the final stanza is an image of merging—where there are no edges, two proximate objects seem one—but whether what are merging are body and body, or body and sea, cannot be determined. Like the poem as a whole, the image is radically ambivalent, both deathly and seductive; as everywhere in Williams, the loss of identity is dangerous, but here it is also mysteriously attractive. The final effect of "The Sea" is one of constantly approaching "statement" without ever being limited to it; the image of the sea which it reflects is fundamentally that of constant change, tension, unfathomable mystery—qualities which the poem brilliantly imitates without betraying them by resolving them.

Williams' development during the late 1920s and 1930s is often described in terms of the principles of the Objectivist movement. The movement itself was extremely loose, consisting in large part of friends of Williams who decided to write the sort of poems Williams had been writing for years. Yet for Williams it signalled an important development in his work, the poem becoming an object in its own right, independent of subjective impressions. Indeed, his comments suggest that the objectivist poem is a version of the transparent lyric as I have defined it, particularly in the rhetorical means by which the poem seeks to engage the reader. Writing for the *Princeton Encyclopedia of Poetry and Poetics*, he stresses the departure from romantic subjectivism. Objectivism is

> a term used to describe a mode of writing, particularly the writing of verse. It recognizes the poem, apart from its meaning, to be an object to be dealt with as such. . . . [Objectivism] concerned itself with an image more particularized yet broadened in its significance. The mind rather than the unsupported eye entered the picture.[25]

And his essay on a collection of Objectivist poetry emphasizes the new relation these poems establish with the reader:

> There is nothing here that seductively leads the sense to
> acceptance by sensuous intrigue. Nor can it be called
> parody since there is no exaggeration or warping for
> false emphasis. Nor is reason used to cudgel the mind
> into unwilling submission. The attack is by simple pre-
> sentation. . . . Each part is similar to, if not identical
> with the moments of the classics by having been scrubbed
> . . . clean of everything adventitious which would make
> poetry a running amusement rather than a constantly
> renewed consistency of contemplation.[26]

Williams' works of this period bring his development of the
transparent lyric to full maturity, often abandoning the notion
of a lyric speaker and moving the reader into the dramatic
center of the poem.

In "The Cod Head" (CEP, 333-34), for example, the point
of view seems to be from underwater; we cannot locate a
single sensibility "apprehending" these details. In contrast to
"The Sea," the poem moves, not through constantly shifting
perspectives, but through accumulation. Its narrow, vertical
shape focuses attention on individual lines and words as dis-
crete objects piled on top of each other; often the lineation
seems so arbitrary ("agitate phosphores- / cent midges") as
to suggest that the downward motion dominates and forces
the form of the poem at the expense of content. The disparate
images from which the poem is composed are not connected
syntactically, but gain cohesion from being juxtaposed. All
these formal qualities mirror the poem's subject: the process
whereby the sea is shaped by the settling of debris and sedi-
ment, and the constant motion of being agitated and settling
again.

The sea in "The Cod Head" is not a restless, dangerous
force, but a passive medium through which forces move; "the
vitreous / body" has no meaning beyond that of the frankly
miscellaneous things it contains. We observe, therefore, not
the sea itself, but those forms and motions that are defined
through its context. The details are observed coolly, dispas-
sionately; there is no more emotion attached to the severed

cod's head than to the red stars or the green stones. Yet the
poem is not purely "objective" or impersonal; everywhere in
it is evidence of an acute intelligence observing, measuring
("four / fathom . . . three fathom"), arranging. In the fol-
lowing passage:

> at night wildly
>
> agitate phosphores-
> cent midges—but by day
> flaccid
>
> moons in whose
> discs sometimes a red cross
> lives—

the word "but" demonstrates the attempt, not only to record,
but to define and order, this world. It signals a consciousness
that discriminates between the jellyfish seen at night as agi-
tated, phosphorescent shimmer, and the same object seen in
the day as a pale, drifting moon, yet recognizes that the sea
can accommodate them both without strain. Unlike the trou-
bled, elusive surface of "The Sea," "The Cod Head" suggests
a world which, beyond all incidental debris, is governed by
a single overriding motion, "a lulling lift / and fall." In order
to understand the poem, the reader must intuit this principle
of order, must construct the particular act of consciousness
out of the poem's distinctive rhythm.

Natural motion also governs "Flowers by the Sea" (CEP,
87), but in this poem it is strikingly enhanced and transformed
by the assertion of imaginative vision:

> When over the flowery, sharp pasture's
> edge, unseen, the salt ocean
>
> lifts its form—chicory and daisies
> tied, released, seem hardly flowers alone
>
> but color and the movement—or the shape
> perhaps—of restlessness, whereas

the sea is circled and sways
peacefully upon its plantlike stem

The poem's surface is cool, elegant, meditative—evoking the
natural scene, perceiving the spatial interplay between the
pasture and the sea, and simultaneously centering on that
process of perception. There is no attempt to describe every
aspect of the scene; rather, the effect is that of capturing and
examining a constellation of motion. But there is no tension
here between natural motion and artistic form, since the poem's
movement illuminates its true subject: the motion of a restless
and imaginative mind. "Flowers by the Sea" consists of a
single complex assertion, yet the source of that assertion is
not localized; the reader must enact the process of perception
in order to turn assertion into authentic vision.

The consciousness embodied in the poem confronts the
landscape, abstracts from it qualities of color and form, threads
its way through paradoxes and ontological questions, and
resolves them into the final peaceful and organic image. The
central conceit reverses the usual opposition between the sta-
bility of the land and the turbulence of the sea: here the sea
has a single form which can be lifted, while the land is seen
only in terms of the blowing flowers, "the movement—or
the shape / perhaps—of restlessness." But more subtly,
throughout the poem the syntax itself raises paradoxes which
are then almost immediately resolved. How can the pasture
be sharp? (It is the pasture's *edge*.) How can we know what
the ocean does if it is unseen? (Unseen itself, it lifts its "form"
over the pasture's edge.) How can the flowers be tied and
released at the same time? (They aren't; the sequence of verbs
imitates the process of motion.) Like the chicory and daisies,
meaning in the poem is alternately tied and released; this play-
ful, restless quality is obviously crucial. Yet the consciousness
represented in the poem never loses its balance. Though the
voice is free to correct itself in mid-statement ("the move-
ment—or the shape / perhaps"), its syntax is immaculate and
sustained. And "seem" is the keyword: the poem never mis-

takes its imaginative vision for the "objective" scene with
which it begins. As much as anything else, the poem celebrates
the pleasures of perception, imagination, and expression; the
fact that the sea—which throughout the poem is seen in con-
trast to the restless flowers—is described in the last couplet
as swaying "peacefully upon its plantlike stem" is an emblem
of the power of the imagination to establish equilibrium, to
unify the world, for the moment when the vision is achieved.

   A poem like "Nantucket" (CEP, 348) makes very different
but equally crucial demands; rather than requiring the reader
to turn a carefully modulated statement into imaginative ex-
perience, it presents no overt statement at all. At the extreme
of Williams' Objectivism, the poem simply offers a list of
images, lacking even the connective rhythms and discrimi-
nations of "The Cod Head":

> Flowers through the window
> lavender and yellow
>
> changed by white curtains—
> Smell of cleanliness—
>
> Sunshine of late afternoon—
> On the glass tray
>
> a glass pitcher, the tumbler
> turned down, by which
>
> a key is lying—And the
> immaculate white bed

The scene exists in perfect equilibrium, divided into its com-
ponent parts which are presented in sequence and with com-
plete objectivity. The act of reading the poem is the opposite
process from the act of writing it; we must reassemble the
elements into a coherent whole—or rather, by responding to
them directly and subjectively, we allow them to express their
own coherence. In recognizing the degree to which the inner
and outer landscapes play off each other, the light and pure
color of nature reinforcing the whiteness and clarity of the

domestic objects, we allow the luminous beauty, the "radiant gist" (P, 186) at the core of all experience, to be revealed.

Yet another version of the transparent lyric as field of action is represented in an extreme form by "The Locust Tree in Flower" (CEP, 93):

> Among
> of
> green
>
> stiff
> old
> bright
>
> broken
> branch
> come
>
> white
> sweet
> May
>
> again

This poem differs from "Nantucket" in that it does not present an overt statement about its subject, but its method of presentation is similar: we confront a series of discrete words (rather than images) for which we must supply coherence. The radical strategy of "The Locust Tree" works to frustrate appeals to conventional systems of order. The title suggests a coherent portrait, but the expectation is immediately undermined. Placing each word on a separate line fragments the portrait, suggests that each word is an equally important unit, and forces us to regard them not as the transparent communicators of conventional discourse, but as opaque and independent objects: "the poem is made of things—on a field" (A, 333). Thirteen ordinary words out of context thus evoke considerable attention to the arbitrary nature of language itself.

The poem is made even more striking by its frustration of

the conventions of syntax. "Among" signals the beginning
of a dependent prepositional phrase, but it is followed not by
the object that would fulfill it but by another preposition, and
then by five contradictory adjectives. The noun that follows,
"branch," is not the plural forecast by "among," nor has it
been introduced by an article, and the (apparently) plural verb
that follows has no appropriate subject. The peculiarly dis-
located syntax defeats the attempt to reassemble the elements
as a lyric speaker's statement. As the sequential logic of gram-
mar is withheld, we are forced to perceive all the words sus-
pended in a continuous present, outside the temporal or causal
relationships implied by conventional speech. At the same
time, of course, the symbolic significance of the words does
assert itself, and while we struggle to maintain linguistic logic
the imaginative vision of the scene emerges. Just as the sweet
white flowers of spring emerge from the locust's stiff branch,
the imagination redeems meaning and wholeness from the
resistance of the verbal field. Although the particular tech-
nique of this poem is not representative, the relation it estab-
lishes with the reader, and the approach to reading poetry it
requires, are fundamental to Williams' work through the rest
of his career.

Finally, "The Sea-Elephant" (CEP, 71-73) represents one
more kind of transparent lyric. Again fragmentation and jux-
taposition are the dominant techniques, but here the elements
are not images or individual words but various voices. The
poem is not a dramatic lyric, since the subjective utterances
are treated as objects, and are assembled and controlled by a
central consciousness that is not dramatically defined. It moves
toward cohesive, organic statement, not through apparent
design and manipulation, but through accumulation, as though
through a willingness to let the details themselves control the
movement. In its lively attention to details and in its allusive,
fragmented, circumlocutory meditation on them, it is one of
Williams' most engaging evocations of the act of the mind.

The poem is difficult for a number of reasons: there are
four voices represented; the primary object, the sea-elephant,

is viewed from various perspectives; the shifting syntactical planes constantly blur the distinction between subject and object. But this shifting and blurring is precisely the point, for through it the poem enacts the process it describes: that of transformation and its relation to perception. It begins with an image of change: the sea-elephant has been transplanted from the strange, heavenlike world of the sea into the human world where beasts are "trundled" rather than swim. The objective central consciousness throughout the poem is characterized by its humor, generosity, wonder. But in the next stanza either the voice of the carnival barker breaks in, or the meditative "voice" imitates him; suddenly the beast is no longer an image of otherworldly wonder, but a monster advertised for its size and the fact that it is alive. Its stupid, gluttonous grossness is mocked ("O wallow / of flesh"), if affectionately.

Abruptly, in the fifth stanza the voice shifts back into a lyric meditation which has nothing ostensibly to do with the sea-elephant. It is linked to the previous stanza by association; the sea-elephant's enormous appetite suggests a kind of seasonal appetite, an impatience for change:

> Sick
> of April's smallness
> the little
> leaves—

and presumably the sentence would be completed in an image of growth. But again the focus shifts (and all this happens nearly instantaneously: not a clear perception, but a fragmented intuition), back to the sea-elephant and its longing for the sea: "Flesh has lief of you / enormous sea." The archaic construction establishes an important motif, presumably signaling intuition of the animal's desire, since when we do hear its actual speech ("Blouaugh!"), it is in seal-language which in turn needs translation ("feed / me"). But immediately thereafter—in the middle of a line whose syntax ["me) my"] sparks the transition—the voice shifts from that of objective translation of the sea-elephant's fleshly appetite to sympathetic expression of its anguish. The whole sequence moves as follows:

> Flesh has lief of you
> enormous sea—
> Speak!
> Blouaugh! (feed
>
> me) my
> flesh is riven—.

The archaic language ("riven") again identifies the utterance with the seal, yet since we have just heard its actual speech ("Blouaugh!") we recognize the transformation taking place: through a sort of ventriloquial sea-change, the voice *becomes* that of the sea-elephant, totally confounding subject and object. But almost before this can be assimilated, the voice is back at a distance, first perceiving the seal's gluttony:

> fish after fish into his maw
> unswallowing
>
> to let them glide down
> gulching back
> half spittle half
> brine

(the lineation constantly forcing attention to the fact that the poem is not merely mirroring experience, but shaping its own form), and then pointing out the pathos:

> the
> troubled eyes—torn
> from the sea.

A "practical voice" breaks in, jolting us from communion with the seal: "They / ought / to put it back where / it came from." In the next three stanzas the consciousness shifts into a reverie which conflates the crowd presently gaping at the sea-elephant with those sailors "back where / it came from,"

for whom its appearance ("rising / bearded / to the surface")
was a strange and noumenal event.

                          —and
            the only
            sense out of them

—out of the sailors? No, out of the gaping crowd—

            is that woman's

—that woman's sense? Is he perhaps thinking of the seals
sailors mistook for mermaids? No, that woman's

            Yes
            it's wonderful but they
            ought to

            put it
            back into the sea where
            it came from.

    The tension which has been established between objective
description and sympathetic participation increases through-
out the rest of the poem; the consciousness moves constantly
into and then away from the seal. Its bellowing again demands
attention, and the following stanza seems clearly a series of
commands addressed to it:

            Swing—ride
            walk
            on wires—toss balls
            stoop and. . . .

But there is something peculiar about this list (How trained
can a trained seal be? "Walk / on wires"? "Stoop"?), and the
next line clarifies the perspective:

            contort yourselves—
            But I
            am love. I am
            from the sea—.

This is the sea-elephant speaking, assuming an authority at once comic, pathetic, and eerie ("I / am love": is it some erotic marine god fished up and trundled here by mistake?). Here the voice seems to go beyond description of the seal's gluttony or evocation of the pain in its eyes; it merges imaginatively with it, and expresses a knowledge and power which do not depend on any external evidence. The third "Blouaugh!" seems to come simultaneously from seal and perceiver, introducing the statement that follows:

> there is no crime save
> the too-heavy
> body
>
> the sea
> held playfully.

The primary meaning seems to center in "held," whose tense emphasizes the contrast between the seal's former "playful" freedom and its present isolation; the crime is in its captivity. And suddenly in mid-sentence the sea-elephant is liberated; past becomes present through the observer's sympathetic imagination. We seem to move away from the seal in a description that is wonderfully vital and fertile:

> —comes
> to the surface
> the water
>
> boiling
> about the head the cows
> scattering
> fish dripping from
>
> the bounty
> of. . . .

—and yet of course the description has this vitality only because we are *not* at a distance, but have entered the animal's predicament completely. This is not "a practical voice" which

merely indicts the seal's captivity, but one that invents and
actualizes its freedom. And in a brilliant final stroke, the last
line echoes the seasonal appetite of the fifth stanza; but whereas
there the image signaled a move away from the immediate
context of the seal, here it assumes the archaic language we
have come to associate with the animal, thus perhaps hinting
at a complete reversal, the sensibility of the seal entering and
expressing the central consciousness:

> and spring
> they say
> Spring is icummen in—

The particularly literary associations of the line suggest even
wilder flights of fancy: the language of the poem itself being
liberated, returning to its origins, "back where / it came from"
(and this evocation would justify retrospectively the seem-
ingly arbitrary translation of seal-language into archaisms).
At any rate, the end of the poem clearly signals a triumph of
the imagination. Although we must avoid enclosing "The
Sea-Elephant" in too small a tank, surely it works on one
level symbolically. Its careful balances and mental leaps em-
body that delicate relationship Williams always insisted the
imagination must maintain with the world. And through the
form of the transparent lyric Williams ensures that the reader's
imagination is immediately and vitally involved.

6

Only the Dance

Here is one at least of this world, moving to meet that other
which is straining for release under my confining ribs—not
wishing so much to understand it as to taste, perhaps, its
freshness—Its freshness!

Williams, *In the American Grain*

But only the dance is sure!
make it your own.
Who can tell
what is to come of it?

in the woods of your
own nature whatever
twig interposes, and bare twigs
have an actuality of their own

this flurry of the storm
that holds us,
plays with us and discards us
dancing, dancing as may be credible.

"The Dance"

The strategies of the transparent lyric, and of the variations I
have described in the previous chapter, remain fundamental
to the development of Williams' work throughout the final
twenty-five years of his career, though they must be seen in
the context of some widely divergent tendencies. *Paterson*, his
great work of the 1940s, exemplifies these tendencies. On one

hand, its inconclusiveness, its formal discontinuities and ap-
parent randomness, its refusal to control or subordinate its
material to neat architectonic ends, all force the reader to
assume an important role in the quest to assimilate and un-
derstand the experience it offers, as in the transparent lyric.
On the other hand, as Marjorie Perloff has convincingly ar-
gued, *Paterson* is at the core a Symbolist text, elaborated on
a firmly dialectical superstructure, "in fact, a much more 'closed'
poem than either Williams or his best critics care to admit."[1]
The relation between the poem's active, fragmented surface
and its careful thematic organization is complex and chal-
lenging; Perloff's analysis will doubtless cause it to receive
more attention, and deservedly so. Yet I propose to pass over
Paterson, and to focus instead in this chapter on the poems
from the final phase of Williams' life, which seem to me to
move again away from Symbolism and toward a renewed
interest in transparence. Perhaps because the challenges *Pat-
erson* presents to the reader are so obvious, critics have made
considerable progress in discovering how to read it; on the
other hand, while the late poems are widely admired, they
have not been explored as carefully. This neglect results, I
believe, from certain widespread general assumptions about
the poems, assumptions that deserve to be questioned.

The poems written in Williams' last decade and collected
in *The Desert Music* (1954), *Journey to Love* (1955), and *Pictures
from Breughel* (1963) share significant departures from his ear-
lier work. Many critics have noted a pervasive shift of manner
and style in the late poems, "an easy, measured grace, a tone
of relaxed assurance, tenderness and benignity of feeling, a
manner that is openly discursive and personal."[2] What is often
remarked is that Williams seems to turn away from the prin-
ciples of objectivism; as Linda Wagner says, "these poems are
primarily expressions of the poet's feelings; the element of
objective description is secondary."[3] And Thomas Whitaker
observes that "more explicitly than ever before, he is impelled
to confess and celebrate . . . in his own person. . . . A ret-
rospective Williams, abandoning strategies of objectification

and speaking out directly, becomes vulnerable to compla-
cency and false naiveté."⁴ A number of reasons have been
adduced for this shift in attitude, most often the aftereffects
of Williams' first two strokes, the second of which brought
him very near death. In a letter written shortly afterward, on
May 27, 1951, he emphasizes his present effort "to state clearly
enough, articulately enough, what I have to say," and con-
tinues: "I must now . . . make myself clear. I must gather
together the stray ends of what I have been thinking and make
my full statement as to their meaning or quit" (SL, 298). The
urge to articulate ideas had always been balanced in Williams'
work by the urge to experience the world directly, but the
specter of old age and death brought him unmistakably closer
to the desire to distill that experience for his readers. It might
also be said that the complex conjunction of life and art that
Williams evolved in *Paterson* led inevitably to poems that drew
more openly on his own life and opinions than the earlier
poems. If, as Williams believed and *Paterson* demonstrates,
nothing was to be excluded as possible subject matter for
poetry, then surely this must include the poet's subjective
judgments and didactic impulses.

Williams never seems to have considered that this new dis-
cursiveness and subjectivity threatened to subvert the control
and discipline that had always been the source of his imagi-
native power. But as James Breslin says, "the new looseness
of manner and tenderness of feeling can sometimes sink into
the sort of soggy, uplifting didacticism that had prompted
Imagism in the first place."⁵ His obsessive emphasis on mat-
ters of prosody—the triadic line and the variable foot—sug-
gests the recognition (whether conscious or not) that he needed
to find new ways of measuring and controlling his subjects,
yet the poems in triadic stanzas include some of the most
romantic and sentimental he ever wrote. It is perhaps also
worth noting that the personal image many of the poems
project—"a benevolent old man, recovering from some near
fatal illness, now filled with love, blessing all he sees, humbly
dispensing wisdom"⁶—is apparently to some extent invented

rather than transcribed from life, since the evidence of the
letters suggests that at this time Williams was often deeply
depressed and drawn towards death.[7] Yet surely no reader
experiences these poems as dramatically distanced from their
author. Williams is always an uneven poet, a condition made
inevitable by the risks to which he was philosophically com-
mitted, but the late poems include some of the least inventive
efforts of his mature work.

The critics seem largely agreed, for example, that "Aspho-
del, That Greeny Flower" is the greatest of Williams' late
poems, but despite moving sections, I find it deeply flawed
by such baggy passages as the following:

                          Having your love
        I was rich.
                 Thinking to have lost it
                          I am tortured
        and cannot rest.
                 I do not come to you
                          abjectly
        with confessions of my faults,
                 I have confessed,
                          all of them.
        In the name of love
                 I come proudly
                          as to an equal
        to be forgiven.
                          (PB, 170-71)

"Asphodel" is more obviously Symbolist than *Paterson*; as
Paul Mariani suggests, it manifests "a complex and highly
organized design around a handful of symbols . . . a design
of mathematical purity and a calculus of persuasions."[8] This
is not in itself a defect, of course, but for me the effect of the
discursive language and traditional design is to blunt the imag-
inative edge demonstrated by Williams' best work. Breslin,
who admires the poem, says that the effect of the discursive-
ness is "to ease the reader's movement through the verse. . . .

Relations here emerge as more important than discrete ob-
jects, and these relations are often articulated at the surface of
the poetry,"[9] and that this new accessibility accounts for the
greater critical popularity of the 1950s poems. This judgment
seems to me to be accurate, yet not to prove the superiority
of the discursive poems. One critic says about "Asphodel,"
for instance, "So that the poem can represent the movement
of a consciousness, it must include much first-person com-
ment, as this does";[10] this is plainly to ignore the resources
of the transparent lyric as Williams used it throughout his
career to represent the process of consciousness without cen-
tering it subjectively.

It is my feeling that the best of the late poems are not those
made more accessible through Williams' new subjectivity, but
those remaining in the tradition of the transparent lyric. This
is not to argue dogmatically for consistency, but rather to
claim that the aesthetic and philosophical resources of this
form comprise Williams' greatest achievement, from which
many of the late poems represent a falling off. Critics have
generally failed to note that discursiveness is not uniform
among the late poems, and that in many of them the mode
of presentation is much the same as in the earlier poems.[11]
The best poems in the late volumes achieve a dramatic dialectic
by playing the techniques of objectivism off against the ten-
derness and grace of Williams' mature vision. Thomas Whi-
taker describes the risks these poems take, and then comments:

> Yet the finest poems succeed not only against such odds
> but because of them. Their speaker, paying attention to
> the temptations of his present moment, may incorporate
> them in the poem's dramatic substance. Such poetry
> works with the most difficult material: the personal
> statement, confessional and celebratory. But in doing
> so, it moves beyond self-consciousness and disarming
> ease into a defenseless honesty of style.[12]

Perhaps because of the "disarming ease" of so many of the
late poems, subsequent criticism has failed to follow up Whit-

aker's suggestion with a careful investigation of their stylistic
strategies. By examining a group of the most successful, I
hope to show that in subtlety and complexity they are the
equal of anything Williams ever wrote.

"Shadows" (PB, 150-52) is a fine example of Williams'
adaptation of the transparent lyric to the ends of his late work.
It is almost wholly composed of ideas, and proceeds through
a chain of direct, discursive statements rather than through a
series of objectively perceived images. Yet "Shadows" is a
version of transparent lyric, since its true center is the act of
the mind that assembles these statements into a coherent vi-
sion. We confront, not a unified idea to which we are expected
simply to assent, but a complex pattern of perceptions and
associations which we must trace out and enact before we can
understand. In essence, the poem reflects objectivist technique
because its reader confronts ideas *as* objects, just as the reader
of "Nantucket" and "The Locust Tree in Flower" confronts
images and single words, respectively, as objects, and is sim-
ilarly required to engage in an exercise in vision. The tech-
nique seems particularly appropriate to a poem whose subject
is perspective, both spatial and temporal, and which estab-
lishes a dialectic between objects perceived directly and ex-
perience transformed by the imagination. The double nature
of the central figure is similarly appropriate: shadows are patches
of darkness thrown by a light source, and serve to define
objects by their absence. The poem weaves a complex texture
of light and dark, presence and absence. To trace its associ-
ations requires the same sort of alertness to disparate values
that the poem discusses.

The opening forces attention to a continually shifting per-
spective:

> Shadows cast by the street light
> under the stars,
> the head is tilted back,
> the long shadow of the legs
> presumes a world

> taken for granted
> on which the cricket trills.
> The hollows of the eyes
> are unpeopled.

Cast syntactically as a single statement, the first sentence is in fact composed of discrete observations linked by association rather than logic. The grammar straddles the line between personal experience and generalization ("the head" rather than "my head"), allowing the reader immediate access to the experience (thus the poem itself is "unpeopled"). And when we project ourselves into the scene we find our attention constantly redirected: from the ground (where presumably the shadows fall) to the light that casts them, to the stars (which dwarf the street light as a light source), to the head (our head, tilted back, looking at the stars), back to the shadows on the ground, and then to the generalization about the world which is the ground for those shadows, and which the sentence is ostensibly intended to express. At the same time that we experience these impressions in sequence, we recognize that they compose a constellation in which they are all true simultaneously, and this perception is pursued in the lines that follow:

> Right and left
> climb the ladders of night
> as dawn races
> to put out the stars.
> That
> is the poetic figure
> but we know
> better: what is not now
> will never
> be. . . .

The double contrast between presence and absence is extended. Just as the voice moves self-consciously to contradict its own "poetic figure" because it is untrue to experience, the

poem's earlier equation between sequence and simultaneity is
qualified by the statement that whatever does not exist now,
in the present moment, will never exist, since the future never
becomes present. Then, in a subtle reversal, the present be-
comes future:

> . . . Sleep secure,
> the little dog in the snapshot
> keeps his shrewd eyes
> pared. Memory
> is liver than sight.

Williams' little joke has a serious point: while the little dog
in the snapshot does not make a very effective watchdog, he
is in a sense a reason for sleeping securely, since the snapshot
(and memory, for which it stands) is a way of preserving the
present that would otherwise slip away. Memory is liver than
sight simply because it makes the absent past present, while
sight (a function only of the present) dies once the moment
is past. The poem then turns on itself once again, moving
from the level of generalization back to the scene in which it
began:

> A man
> looking out,
> seeing the shadows—
> it is himself
> that can be painlessly amputated
> by a mere shifting
> of the stars.
> A comfort so easily not to be
> and to be at once one
> with every man.

The man, who has presumably come to represent the reader,
looks out not from the security of a snapshot but from the
vulnerability of the moment, and recognizes that experience
in a world taken for granted is in fact ephemeral, that shadows
are the record of an object's absence as well as of its presence.

Yet to see human life so reduced in perspective is in a way
comforting, since it enforces a sense of unity with all others.
On this note, the poem rises to a lyric pitch that reflects both
this notion of wholeness and a celebration of the darkness that
underlies it:

        The night blossoms
                with a thousand shadows
                        so long
            as there are stars,
                    street lights
                            or a moon and
            who shall say
                    by their shadows
            which is different
                    from the other
                            fat or lean.

    The second section of the poem opens in a less complex
way:

        Ripped from the concept of our lives
                and from all concept
                        somehow, and plainly,
            the sun will come up
                    each morning
                            and sink again.
            So that we experience
                    violently
                            every day
            two worlds
                    one of which we share with the
                    rose in bloom
                            and one,
            by far the greater,
                    with the past,
                            the world of memory,

> the silly world of history,
> the world
> of the imagination.

The spectral, nighttime world of shadows gives way to sun
and day, but the world of nature is still markedly independent
of human understanding and aspiration. The double con-
sciousness of the first section is also extended; the world of
present experience, represented by the rose in bloom (echoing
the blossoming shadows of night), is in turn framed by the
world of memory and imagination, and both these worlds
make up our violent daily experience. There follows the sort
of associative shift that makes "Shadows" a transparent lyric
rather than a dramatic meditation:

> Which leaves only the beasts and trees,
> crystals
> with their refractive
> surfaces
> and rotting things
> to stir our wonder.
> Save for the little
> central hole
> of the eye itself
> into which
> we dare not stare too hard
> or we are lost.

The passage is constructed on a syllogistic model (proposition:
so that . . .: which leaves . . .: save for . . .), yet its logic is
not clear and precise but elliptical and associative. Behind the
rhetoric of argument, the attention—both that which informs
the voice of the poem and that of the reader—searches out
wanderingly the truth of this experience. Why does the double
perspective leave us these things to stir our wonder? (They
are the stuff of present experience and at the same time acquire
meaning through memory and imagination.) Why "only"
these things? (The word is ironic; animal, vegetable, and min-

eral, they comprise the entire objective world.) The subjective world also inspires wonder, of course, yet too much introspection risks loss of the immediate objective moment and absorption into the world of shadows. The eerily impersonal, "unpeopled" "hole of the eye" achieves a double perspective, so that we find ourselves both staring in and stared into at once. And then, in a final stroke, the poem finds perfect resolution:

> The instant
> trivial as it is
> is all we have
> unless—unless
> things the imagination feeds upon,
> the scent of the rose,
> startle us anew.

This is not simply a discursive statement; the rhythms of discovery—the sudden turn in mid-sentence, the compulsive repetition of "unless," the unstudied apposition of the scent to things, and the wonderful figure of the imagination feeding beelike on *the* scent of *the* rose, both generic and individual at the same time—allow us to internalize it as immediate experience. The two worlds converge, apparently as naturally and spontaneously as the poem says they do. By forcing us to recognize the measured indirections behind the discursive statements, the poem enacts the dual perspective that is its subject.

Typical of the ways in which Williams uses objectivist technique to modify or qualify subjective vision are poems that rely heavily on lineation and punctuation (or the lack of it) to displace the discursive voice into a new composition. Written in prose and conventionally punctuated, "Iris" (PB, 30), for example, could almost represent a natural declarative sentence.[13] (It is, of course, not a complete sentence, and the fragmented, exclamatory first line contributes importantly to its effect.) Yet as Williams lineates it and breaks it into stanzas, the statement produces an entirely different effect:

a burst of iris so that
come down for
breakfast

we searched through the
rooms for
that

sweetest odor and at
first could not
find its

source then a blue as
of the sea
struck

startling us from among
those trumpeting
petals

The shape of the stanza asserts itself as the dominant principle
of the poem; the simple domestic incident has been poured
into a mold it seems obviously not to fit. The length of the
lines does not correspond to natural units of attention, and as
we begin to read the poem our attention strains uncomfortably
to reject the arbitrary, to join "for" and "breakfast," "the"
and "rooms," and to pause between "odor" and "and." This
formal tension makes reading the poem an entirely different
experience from that of simply hearing the incident recounted;
it makes us conscious of the composition as an entity separate
from the persona whose voice we ostensibly hear. In this way,
the poem may be seen as a near-relation of the transparent
lyric, even though it is grounded in the experience of a dra-
matized speaker.

Perhaps the most subtle effect comes in the penultimate
stanza. Each previous stanza has ended without closure, the
syntax catapulting us into the next. Suddenly, at the moment
when the iris is discovered, the single word "struck" gets a
line to itself and ends both the clause and the stanza, thus

merging the poem's statement with its "arbitrary" form in
an emphatic "sudden rightness," as Stevens would call it. The
clarity and impact of the fairly simple metaphor (a color strik-
ing—considerably more interesting than a "striking color")
give way in the following stanza to a pleasant confusion (it
seems at first as though "we" are startled from among the
petals rather than that the color emanates from them) and
synaesthesia (the source of an *odor* is finally *sighted* in the
trumpeting petals). And appropriate enough in a poem that
begins in mystery and ends in celebration, the clause of the
last stanza, although again broken by the lineation, is much
more strongly cadenced than the earlier stanzas. Partly because
of the emphatic repetition of "ng" sounds, and partly because
we have simply grown accustomed to the stanzaic pattern,
the final line breaks seem inevitable rather than disconcerting.
Thus even the apparently simple late lyrics often draw on
complex strategies of style, and are not the simple transcrip-
tions of sentiment they are sometimes taken to be.

"Portrait of a Woman at Her Bath" (PB, 46) also expresses
the subjective feelings of a dramatized persona, an "I" with
a bathing woman in his house, yet again that self-expression
is displaced by the poem's formal texture:

> it is a satisfaction
> a joy
> to have one of those
> in the house
>
> when she takes a bath
> she unclothes
> herself she is no
> Venus
>
> I laugh at her
> an Inca
> shivering at the well
> the sun is

> glad of a fellow to
> marvel at
> the birds and the flowers
> look in

The stanzas assume a regular length and shape, but here these features do not seem arbitrary; in fact, the immediate impression is that each line does reflect a unit of attention, and that the shape of the stanza deliberately attends to what it says. The central tension is rather between the composed, painterly connotations of the title and the casual, seemingly spontaneous rhythms and movement of the poem itself. In the context of a simple, straightforward celebration of natural beauty, Williams constructs a series of confusions between the real and the imagined. The first of these is the title itself: we cannot know whether what we are about to read is the response to a painting (in the manner of the "Pictures from Breughel") or is itself the portrait—in other words, whether the poem is modeled on art or on life. This ambiguity is apparently resolved in the first stanza: surely the tone of "satisfaction" and the implication of ownership reflect a painting and not an actual woman. But in the next stanza the focus on process and the contrast with Venus (evoking such representations as Botticelli's and the Venus de Milo) suggest life rather than art as the model—unless of course the act of unclothing takes place in the speaker's imagination. The question remains an active one through the rest of the poem, as the speaker builds a complex response to the woman's unidealized body. His laughing at her while she stands shivering might seem self-consciously cruel were it not clear that what he is really laughing at is his own apt analogy. And in the relaxed whimsy that follows, as the sun, birds, and flowers are personified and made a part of a cartoonish composition focused on the woman, the distinction between the worlds of art and nature is blurred. Whether or not the poem is based on a painting, it does itself finally become a portrait, not the formal composition by Renoir or Degas suggested by the title, but an animated cartoon.

The measure of Williams' control of tone is that the woman is not similarly reduced; his praise of her as fellow to the sun is seriously based, and he pulls the poem back from exaggerated encomium by having the birds and flowers "look in," framing the subject rather than adorning her with garlands of praise. Again, this subtle pattern of formal tension and resolution brings the poem close to the model of the transparent lyric, since it displaces the subjective statement as the center of the reading experience.

The formal tensions in "Chloe" (PB, 50-51) are of a different sort, but they serve much the same purpose. The poem captures the complex movement of the attention confronting a series of objects by juxtaposing images at the expense of conventional syntax. The speaker's purpose is twofold, both to relate an incident and to indulge himself in a moment of generalized meditation; the movement is thus both linear and circular at the same time, which leads the reader through a labyrinth of possible turnings in order to search out the meaning. In one sense this distances the reader from the speaker, in the mode of the dramatic lyric, but since the reader must work toward seeing the experience as the speaker sees it in order to comprehend it, it also brings them together. The syntax, in other words, is predicated on an assumption of shared knowledge and interiority, rather than calculated for communication, and in order to get past initial confusion, the reader must sort out the syntax and share those assumptions.

Here is the poem:

> The calves of
> the young girls legs
> when they are well made
>
> knees
> lithely built
> in their summer clothes
>
> show them
> predisposed toward flight
> or the dance

> the magenta flower
> of the
> moth-mullen balanced
>
> idly
> tilting her weight
> from one foot
>
> to the other
> shifting
> to avoid looking at me
>
> on my way to
> mail a letter
> smiling to a friend

Aside from the absence of the possessive apostrophe ("girls"), the first stanza is perfectly straightforward; it establishes a general subject—despite the specificity of the title—and forecasts a predicate for "calves." But immediately the second stanza subverts our expectations by providing not a verb but another noun clause, forcing us to consider that the poem may be constructed as a series of images rather than as a syntactical whole. Yet as an independent unit this clause is suspicious; although "knees lithely built" is peculiar but understandable, "knees in their summer clothes" is bizarre, particularly since knees are distinctly unclothed in summer. Surely the "their" refers back to "girls," and suggests a stronger syntactical link between the stanzas than that of a series. And the third stanza provides that link by supplying the verb required by the first stanza and framing the second as an interjected, if oddly constructed, phrase. The consciousness so far projected is relaxed and detached, willing to break the direct line of meditation in order to embellish it, and observing the girls generically, at a genial distance.

With the fourth stanza, the unpunctuated line breaks abruptly: the image of the mullen flower is simply juxtaposed to what precedes it, implying a simile without supplying one, thus forcing the reader to supply the analogy that links the images.

The first three stanzas have all represented units of attention; this leads us to assume that "balanced" modifies "flower," and that it will be completed in the next stanza by a phrase like "atop the stalk." But moving into the fifth stanza, we realize that a complex and subtle shift has taken place, and that the referent is no longer the flower, not the general "young girls" of the first stanza, but the specific girl named in the title. It is impossible to identify exactly where this shift occurs, and the result is a delicate suspension in which the natural balances of moth-mullen, girlhood, and Chloe are all evoked simultaneously as the poem tilts its weight from one foot to the other. And in a further shift, the speaker's true role is gradually revealed. What had seemed a generalized meditation is seen as rooted in localized incident, and the apparent detachment in fact masks considerable involvement in the scene. The "casual" description, into which the poem appears to fall artlessly, precisely defines Chloe's insouciance, and evokes the gap between her idle avoidance of the speaker's gaze and his obviously intent interest in her. In its open syntax and extended present participles, the surface of the closing stanzas preserves the stance of objective detachment. Yet the reader who works out the syntax and the vision can share the subtle tensions that animate it. The final stroke in this process is the last line, which at first appears to refer to the speaker, who is the subject of the rest of the stanza. Imaginative apprehension of the scene, though, reveals that the speaker's attention is entirely on the girl, and that *she* smiles to a friend rather than to him. The poem as a whole does not attempt to define the dynamics between the figures very precisely, choosing rather to provide us minimal data about which we may draw our own conclusions. This is exactly the point of distinction from the dramatic monologue; Williams prefers to lead us into the scene as immediately as possible, rather than to have us view his own staging from a distance.

"The Polar Bear" (PB, 16) at first seems to represent one of the most common romantic forms, a discursive meditation on an object in nature. But to read the poem is an experience altogether different from reading Frost's "The Oven Bird" or Lawrence's "Snake," which attempt to communicate the poets' subjective impressions as though to an auditor. The movement of Williams' poem is so internalized, so intuitive, that it is difficult to say precisely even what its subject is. But as it forces us to adopt its perspective, it provides a vision that is powerfully evocative and mysterious:

> his coat resembles the snow
> deep snow
> the male snow
> which attacks and kills
>
> silently as it falls muffling
> the world
> to sleep that
> the interrupted quiet return
>
> to lie down with us
> its arms
> about our necks
> murderously a little while

The poem opens conventionally, even banally, with a descriptive analogy intended to express the appearance of its ostensible subject. But immediately the syntax loosens and the rhythm breaks: the sentence loops back on itself to explore the image so obsessively that by the end of the stanza the snow has replaced the polar bear as the focus of attention. Or rather, the bear becomes a sort of submerged metaphor expressing itself through the murderous violence of the snow. Normal logic in the form of descriptive simile gives way to irrational vision. Nothing about the bear's coat *requires* the associations that emerge. The second stanza pursues these developments farther. Rather than returning to the description of the bear, it continues within the same sentence to shift the perspective again: the violence of the snow is muffled and merged with sleep. By this point the reader must abandon all expectations about where the poem will lead; in fact, the illusion is that it is not leading at all, but following the un-premeditated course of mind in reverie or dream. In the seventh line, "that" is an extremely ambiguous connective—presumably meaning "in order that," but the syntax here is very loose—and in the next line it is unclear whether "quiet" is an adjective or a noun, and whether "return" is a noun or a verb. To stop and attempt to puzzle these questions out is to assume there is a clear statement one is not "getting." This is precisely the wrong response. The poem works to establish a powerfully imaginative perspective, a vision in which cold and violence and sleep and death are inextricably tied, and the purpose of its stylistic eccentricities is to force us into the world. Thus drawn in, we are apt to find the last stanza both chilling and exhilarating. It is at the same time simple and enormously mysterious, given what precedes it: the "it" whose arms encircle our necks is the quiet, the snow, and even the bear at once, and the death with which it threatens us is also a kind of love and a kind of sleep. By proceeding intuitively and suggestively, Williams involves us in the experience even if we only dimly understand it; indeed, the sense that it can be evoked indirectly seems critical to the paralysis, the hibernation, that gradually emerges as the poem's subject.

Paradigmatic of Williams' treatment of the transparent lyric in his late work is the ironically named "Sonnet in Search of an Author" (PB, 60). Overtly, the title refers to the pressure of the material out of which a poem "might be made" to find an appropriate form; the conceit is that the poem exists as a kind of Platonic essence awaiting an author to bring it to fruition. But as usual in the transparent lyric, there is a counter-movement, in this case the material's urge to *escape* from its author, to evade the subjective idea that binds it and to return to the objectivity of elemental experience. Williams' use of the traditional form to express this dialectic is masterful. The octave expresses the primary idea directly:

> Nude bodies like peeled logs
> sometimes give off a sweetest
> odor, man and woman

under the trees in full excess
matching the cushion of

aromatic pine-drift fallen
threaded with trailing woodbine
a sonnet might be made of it

The opening analogy gives the pastoral scene a distinctly Wil-
liamsesque edge, but the observation remains thoroughly ro-
mantic, a subjective assertion of human and sylvan harmony
that extends itself through seven lines. The eighth line, sug-
gesting that a sonnet be made from this material, is a natural
extension of this mood, given the sonnet's traditional asso-
ciations. Williams' sly joke, of course, is that the sonnet he
is in the process of writing is in most formal respects not
traditional at all. This seems to be acknowledged in the fol-
lowing line, which—although it may be read as simply echo-
ing the idea affirmatively—may also be taken as knowing,
subtle mockery. And following this turn, the sonnet "made"
on this idea begins to disassemble itself:

Might be made of it! odor of excess
odor of pine needles, odor of
peeled logs, odor of no odor
other than trailing woodbine that

has no odor, odor of a nude woman
sometimes, odor of a man.

The affirmation of harmony, the celebration of ripeness, even
the judgment that the man, woman, and pine-drift are aro-
matic, all that composed the impetus for the sonnet subsides,
and we are left with a simple list of smells. The subjective
judgment that articulates metaphor and analogy is superseded
by the pure reality of direct experience—which is at the same
time for the reader deeply evocative. The poem that began
by going in search of an author ends by proving it does not
need one. The whole sonnet acts out in miniature the most
important development of Williams' poetics, the movement

beyond Romantic subjectivism to what Stevens called vivid transparence.

The great achievement of Williams' late poetry is the lyric structures he found to merge openly personal feeling with the techniques of objectivism. Despite critical emphasis on discursiveness and didacticism in the late poems, at his best Williams never surrendered to the excesses of Romantic subjectivism. He found ways of measuring and controlling subjective experience, not by translating it into metaphysical or symbolic structures, but by objectifying it. Like Stevens, Williams sought not to stress the poet's anonymity by adopting fictional masks, and thus enforcing the division between writer and work, but in essence to construct a self *within* the poem by centering it on a process of consciousness or act of vision. The rhetorical strategies by which this is achieved are complex and various, as I have demonstrated, but their effect is to draw the reader into "the poem of the act of the mind" and to allow us to experience the process that composes the poem directly and immediately.

Postscript

Having defined transparence and demonstrated its importance and development in the work of Stevens and Williams, I think it may be useful to ask what general conclusions might be drawn from such a study. My emphasis on close readings of individual poems risks a kind of narrowness, and a skeptical reader might well ask what exactly is to be gained by considering the notion of transparence in modern and contemporary poetry in general. I began by defining the transparent lyric as rhetorically and epistemologically different from the characteristic Romantic forms, but what does the sort of approach I have undertaken here contribute to our understanding of the development of modern poetics? How does acknowledging the quality of transparence help us read modern poems accurately and imaginatively? Two recent critics have been particularly useful to me in the last phases of my work on this book. Their subjects and methodologies are quite different, but taken together they help to define the importance of the kind of poem I have attempted to describe here.

Charles Altieri's *Act and Quality: A Theory of Literary Meaning and Humanistic Understanding*,[1] as the title suggests, is a highly theoretical argument for locating meaning in literary texts by viewing them not as thematic constructs but as performed actions. This "dramatistic" approach to meaning, grounded in action philosophy and structural linguistics, has been highly stimulating for me, particularly in its implications for the relation between authorial acts and dramatic acts within the text. Perhaps even more valuable to me is his use of the performance model to counter the various theorists who claim that all texts are ultimately indeterminant. A Deconstructionist would presumably discount the notion of the transparent lyric, as especially requiring the reader's active participation to achieve its meaning, since for such a critic this is in fact the necessary strategy of any text. To an extent of course this is correct; as Altieri says, "there is a tautological sense in which meaning requires an interpreter, or writers only produce meaning a reader completes, and there is obvious truth in distinguishing between referential and performative discourse" (p. 6). But to conclude further that meanings are therefore radically subjective, indeterminant, and unverifiable is to fail to "address the differences between linguistic possibilities and actual linguistic choices" (p. 229). By viewing texts as performances of actions we can demonstrate that they project a sense of informing purpose; "texts have properties of particularity, dramatic tension, and depth because we construe them as specific performances in situations which unfold in time for our sympathy and reflection" (p. 235). This argument justifies my assumption that determinacy is a relative property of texts, and my discussion of the relation of the transparent lyric to the act of reading it as a dialectical process from which meaning emerges in a particular way.

In light of Altieri's theory, the notion of transparence is most important because it offers an additional model for the way dramatic performance may be accomplished by a text. In an earlier, related essay Altieri states that

a poem can call attention to at least three different forms of conscious action, often in complex combinations: it can present forms of dramatic narrative where the audience is asked to sympathize with the character and to construct the moral and psychological implications of the total action; it can foreground the processes of reflection in a dramatized lyric persona expressing immediate feelings, trying out rhetorical roles, or meditating on a scene, event, or idea; and it can foreground the activity of an implicit author who shows signs of his artistic effort to give form to the flux of experience or tries by manipulating language and structure to incorporate the perspective of his dramatized speaker in a larger, more complex vision. The ballad, the poetry of

Keats, and that of Yeats might be taken as exemplary
of these three strategies.[2]

I believe that the transparent lyric offers a fourth form of
action by foregrounding, not a dramatized speaker, but the
reader himself or herself in the performance of the poem's
conscious action. Reading, in short, requires not simply sym-
pathy or even empathy, but direct participation in order to
fulfill the text's meaning. And through what I have called its
double vision, the transparent lyric offers simultaneously a
self-conscious and aesthetic view of that performance. I would
emphasize that to recognize transparence has a value besides
that of taxonomy. Altieri's view of meanings is ultimately a
social and cultural one; he argues that "the performances in
literary texts may exemplify attitudes which represent pos-
sible ways of acting or making judgments in ordinary expe-
rience," which readers "can project as means of understanding
their own actions, those of others, and the ways culture makes
possible this range of discriminations" (p. 12). Through its
complex rhetorical strategy, through the way its distinctively
unmediated dramatic stance challenges the reader's imagina-
tion to confront the world, the transparent lyric would seem
to be a particularly effective form for achieving these cultural
ends.

Marjorie Perloff's *The Poetics of Indeterminacy*, to which I
have already referred a number of times, is a very different
sort of book, primarily historical and textual rather than the-
oretical. The subject of Perloff's elegant and powerful inquiry
is what she calls " 'the French connection'—the line that goes
from Rimbaud to Stein, Pound, and Williams by way of
Cubist, Dada, and early Surrealist art, a line that also includes
the great French/English verbal compositions of Beckett."
She argues that "Modernism" is constituted of two separate
strands: the Symbolist mode of Yeats and Eliot, inherited
from the Romantics, and the " 'anti-Symbolist' mode of in-
determinacy or 'undecidability,' of literalness and free play,
whose first real exemplar was the Rimbaud of the *Illumina-*

tions" (p. vii). At first glance Perloff's thesis might seem to divide her from Altieri's argument against indeterminacy, but this is not so: she explicitly distinguishes her use of the term from Derrida's (pp. 17-18), meaning by it not a property inevitably shared by all texts, but one manifested by the specific texts she discusses. And in treating "undecidability" as a strategy deliberately adopted by her poets, she demonstrates that the texts are in fact "determinant" in the larger sense defined by Altieri. Both critics agree that "determinacy" is a relative rather than an absolute term, a quality that texts may exhibit to a greater or lesser degree.

In light of Perloff's argument, as I suggested earlier, the particular significance of transparence would seem to be as a bridge between her two traditions. The poems examined in the previous chapters clearly do not demonstrate the sort of radical instability and incoherence Perloff says results in undecidability: "what happens in Pound's *Cantos*, as in Stein's *Tender Buttons* . . . or Beckett's *How It Is* or John Cage's *Silence*, is that the symbolic evocations generated by words on the page are no longer grounded in a coherent discourse, so that it becomes impossible to decide which of these associations are relevant and which are not" (p. 18). Stevens' poems in particular are grounded in a coherent body of ideas and expressed through symbolic patterns of image and color; Williams' poems, while less systematic, also manifest emphatic mythic and psychic structures. At the same time, as I have suggested throughout, their poems demonstrate important rhetorical and dramatic differences from the characteristic work of the Symbolist tradition, differences that serve to challenge the reader in a variety of ways—undermining preconceptions, shifting perspectives, juggling objective and subjective modes—that result in much the same freshness and immediacy that Perloff describes as the goal of indeterminacy. The transparent lyric would thus seem to occupy a highly significant place in the modern aesthetic, one that deserves further attention.

My emphasis on transparence would also serve to modify

two of Perloff's conclusions. One is her view of Williams.
She includes Williams as a member of her "other tradition"
(I elided ". . . or Williams' *Spring and All* . . ." from the
sentence quoted above), though, it turns out, only in a sharply
qualified way. Her chapter about him is subtitled "The 'French'
Decade of William Carlos Williams," and her claim to in-
determinacy in his work is largely confined to *Spring and All*
(1922) and *The Descent of Winter* (1928). Even within *Spring
and All*, her detailed and persuasive readings are restricted to
the angular, Cubist constructions of "The red paper box" and
"Black winds from the north"; I hope I have demonstrated
that such other poems as "By the road to the contagious
hospital" and "The Red Wheelbarrow" exhibit far more co-
herent and less "undecidable" qualities. Perloff's account of
Williams also suggests that after the remarkable experiments
of the 1920s he retreated gradually toward a more coherent
and Symbolist aesthetic, a poetic not finally as congenial to
his imagination. This is a view I largely share, but as my final
chapter maintains, I believe that in his final phase—a period
not treated by Perloff—Williams moved back toward trans-
parence, toward a precision and objectivity that at its best
matched the achievements of forty years earlier.

The notion of transparence as a third tradition would also
modify Perloff's view of Stevens, whom she uses several times
to represent the Modernist/Symbolist position. Her discus-
sion of Canto II of "The Auroras of Autumn" as "squarely
within the Romantic tradition" (p. 21), for instance, is based
entirely on thematic grounds. She assumes that Stevens is
represented by a dramatic persona within the poem: "the min-
imal landscape the poet tries to evade is one of total bareness.
. . . Stevens cannot avoid this autumnal truth" (p. 20), and
so on. But viewed in terms of its rhetorical strategy, the poem
takes on a different cast: there is no "I" in the section, no
dramatized character at the beginning of the section at all,
simply a sequence of starkly objectified perceptions:

Farewell to an idea . . . A cabin stands,
Deserted, on a beach. It is white,
As by custom or according to

An ancestral theme or as a consequence
Of an infinite course. The flowers against the wall
Are white, a little dried, a kind of mark

Reminding, trying to remind, of a white
That was different, something else, last year
Or before, not the white of an aging afternoon,

Whether fresher or duller, whether of winter cloud
Or of winter sky, from the horizon to horizon.
The wind is blowing the sand across the floor.

Here, being visible is being white,
Is being of the solid of white, the accomplishment
Of an extremist in an exercise . . .

                             (CP, 412)

The rhetoric seems even deliberately to evade contact with a specific persona ("Reminding, trying to remind of a white . . ."), and the result, I would claim, is to establish a complex interaction between the narrative and the reader's imagination, which encounters the drift of abstract and concrete sensations, memory and speculation, without the benefit of a mediating consciousness. When the figure of "the man" appears in the seventh stanza, it is not to "resolve" this interaction, but to add one more figure to the calculus—he may in some sense be responsible for the meditation that precedes his entrance, but then again he may not. To reduce this epistemological uncertainty to a thematic interpretation, to argue that because the poem's images can be read as symbolic, "the landscape of 'The Auroras of Autumn' is thus the externalization of the poet's psyche" (p. 22), is to miss much of the uncertainty and instability that Perloff values so highly in other poets. Again, in Altieri's terms, seeing the poem as transparent requires attention to its performance, its particular rhetoric and dramatic stance. And that attention reveals qualities and possibilities even a critic as good as Perloff is apt to overlook.

Finally, a further value of the idea of transparence is as a corrective to certain widespread assumptions about the development of American poetry after the generation of Stevens and Williams. Contemporary poetry is often treated monolithically as the inevitable result of a rhetorical and epistemological tradition established by Whitman and Emerson. I would argue that the phenomenon of transparence itself defines a tradition in recent poetry that is not often adequately recognized. For example, in an influential study of contemporary poetry Ralph J. Mills, Jr., focuses on those writers who, in reaction to what they perceive as the excessive rationality and objectivity of the previous generation, have sought to ground their poems in their own personality and experience, and to communicate by sharing their feelings as openly as possible. He then generalizes: "The contemporary poet recreates himself as a personality, an identifiable self within his poetry . . . not perhaps a full likeness for the author as a physical, workaday person outside the poem yet [who] could not be mistaken for someone else." This poet, according to Mills, "invites us to share in his pursuit of identity; to witness the dramatization of the daily events of his experience—so closely resembling our own; to be haunted by the imagery of his dreams or the flowing stream of his consciousness."³ Mills' description serves very well to characterize those writers on whom he focuses: Robert Lowell, John Berryman, Theodore Roethke, Galway Kinnell, and Philip Levine, among others. But as a general assumption about contemporary poetry it is false and misleading.

One wonders, for instance, what Mills would say about John Ashbery in this context. Ashbery is a particularly interesting example because—though Perloff counts him among her indeterminate poets—he has been so often treated as a direct descendant of the Romantics; Harold Bloom says quite

emphatically, "All of Ashbery . . . is profound self-revela-
tion,"[4] and links him with Shelley and Stevens in a sort of
Sublime Trinity. Indeed, some of Ashbery's description of
his own method makes him sound nearly as profoundly sub-
jective as Bloom claims: "I think that any one of my poems
might be considered to be a snapshot of whatever is going
on in my mind at the time—first of all the desire to write a
poem, after that wondering if I've left the oven on or thinking
about where I must be in the next hour."[5]

Yet to see Ashbery as an "all-but-perfect solipsist" whose
work is "enigmatically autobiographical, even if it were en-
tirely fantasy,"[6] is I think to distort what the experience of
reading the poems is actually like. Elsewhere he describes his
work in considerably less subjective terms:

> It seems to me that my poetry sometimes proceeds as
> though an argument were suddenly derailed and some-
> thing that started out clearly suddenly becomes opaque.
> It's a kind of mimesis of how experience comes to me:
> as one is listening to someone else—a lecturer, for in-
> stance—who's making perfect sense but suddenly slides
> into something that eludes one. What I am probably
> trying to do is to illustrate opacity and how it can sud-
> denly descend over us, rather than trying to be willfully
> obscure.[7]

Even given the characteristic ingenuousness ("What I am
probably trying to do"), it seems clear that in calling his work
mimetic of experience and an illustration of the generalized
sensation of opacity, Ashbery encourages us to see it as some-
thing other than "wholly self-enclosed."[8] This suggestion is
even more pronounced in a 1976 statement: "I don't think
my poetry is inaccessible. People say it's very private, but I
think it's about the privacy of everyone."[9] The wonder of
Ashbery's work, it seems to me, is the ways it finds to use
his extraordinary resources of voice to turn admittedly per-
sonal experience outward, to make the fluid, discontinuous
process of thinking as real and immediate to the reader as to

the poet. In opposition to Mills' model of the poet re-creating "himself as a personality, an identifiable self" who "invites us to share in his pursuit of identity," Ashbery's characteristic strategy is systematically to destroy the notion of an identifiable self in the poem by using the multiplicity of language to undermine our faith in dramatic consistency and identity. The poems' quirky, arbitrary, shifting perspectives serve not to manifest a willful, privileged autonomy, but rather to transform Ashbery's own privacy into "the privacy of everyone."

Here, for example, is Ashbery's "Crazy Weather":

It's this crazy weather we've been having:
Falling forward one minute, lying down the next
Among the loose grasses and soft, white, nameless
    flowers.
People have been making a garment out of it,
Stitching the white of lilacs together with lightning
At some anonymous crossroads. The sky calls
To the deaf earth. The proverbial disarray
Of morning corrects itself as you stand up.
You are wearing a text. The lines
Droop to your shoelaces and I shall never want or
    need
Any other literature than this poetry of mud
And ambitious reminiscences of times when it came
    easily
Through the then woods and ploughed fields and had
A simple unconscious dignity we can never hope to
Approximate now except in narrow ravines nobody
Will inspect where some late sample of the rare,
Uninteresting specimen might still be putting out shoots,
    for all we know.[10]

The poem's charm derives in part from Ashbery's skill at taking the conventions of pastoral—the high compliment, the harmony of nature and art, nostalgia for a Golden Age—and expressing them in the prosy, deadpan irony of contemporary language: "The proverbial disarray / Of morning corrects it-

self as you stand up," "You are wearing a text. The lines /
Droop to your shoelaces," "a simple unconscious dignity we
can never hope to / Approximate now." But "Crazy Weather"
is considerably more than a send-up of the pastoral; it gains
surprising urgency and daffy beauty from its use of the strat-
egies of transparence. What distinguishes this poem from two-
dimensional parody is its refusal to allow the reader the fixed,
knowing perspective on which parody depends. Rather, its
continual shifts in diction, tone, and attitude result in an ex-
perience of perpetual irresolution and imbalance.[11]

   The poem is constructed as a series of distractions; from
the cliché of the first line to its anthropomorphized literali-
zation in the second and third, to its metamorphosis from
subject to object in the fourth, and from the mythic resonance
of the fifth line to the archness of "proverbial disarray," we
experience not the "pursuit of identity," but rather a pro-
gression of false-bottomed Chinese boxes. As a result, we
lose any sense of a consistent dramatic speaker, even of the
stream of consciousness of one, and the uncertainty and be-
wilderment—the "crazy weather"—the poem enacts become
ours in the act of reading. And thus the modest, hedging
acknowledgment of the possibility of dignity that emerges at
the end of that last meandering sentence ("'some late sample
of the rare, / Uninteresting specimen might still be putting
out shoots, for all we know") acquires an unexpected radi-
ance. As the convention of the identifiable lyric speaker dis-
solves, we find ourselves in the narrow ravine, searching for
the specimen in a peculiarly immediate way.

   Ashbery's manner is, of course, highly idiosyncratic, but
his underlying strategy—using the rhetoric of transparence to
turn personal experience outward and make it immediately
accessible to the reader—is not. He describes the dialectic
himself as follows:

   The extreme austerity of an almost empty mind
   Colliding with the lush, Rousseau-like foliage of its
      desire to communicate

Something between breaths, if only for the sake
Of others and their desire to understand you and
    desert you
For other centers of communication, so that
    understanding
May begin, and in doing so be undone.[12]

The range of rhetorical modes in contemporary poetry is wider
than is sometimes recognized. Expressionistic or neo-Freud-
ian accounts do not often deal adequately with those poets
like Ashbery who seek to communicate not by making *them-
selves* more accessible, but by constructing the poem as a
process of invention and discovery through which the reader
comes to view the world in a particular way. A short list of
current American practitioners would include poets as various
as Charles Simic, Mark Strand, Sandra McPherson, Charles
Wright, David St. John, Laura Jensen, W. S. Merwin, and
Dennis Schmitz.

The transparent lyric is alive and well. Its tradition, as I
have defined it here in terms of Stevens and Williams, con-
stitutes an important and continuing response to what Wil-
liams calls in *Spring and All* the "bitter and delicious relations"
between subject and object, self and world.

Notes

PREFACE

1. Monroe C. Beardsley, *The Possibility of Criticism* (Detroit: Wayne State University Press, 1970), p. 101.
2. Wallace Stevens, *The Collected Poems of Wallace Stevens* (New York: Knopf, 1954), p. 460.
3. John Reichert, *Making Sense of Literature* (Chicago: University of Chicago Press, 1977), p. 17. Reichert significantly modifies this position in his "Do Poets Ever Mean What They Say?" *New Literary History* 13 (1981), 53–68.
4. William Carlos Williams, *Collected Earlier Poems* (New York: New Directions, 1951), p. 93.
5. Wolfgang Iser, *The Implied Reader: Patterns of Communication in Prose Fiction from Bunyon to Beckett* (Baltimore: Johns Hopkins University Press, 1974), pp. 274–75. See also Umberto Eco, *The Role of the Reader: Explorations in the Semiotics of Texts* (Bloomington: Indiana University Press, 1979); and Susan R. Suleiman and Inge Crosman, eds., *The Reader in the Text: Essays on Audience and Interpretation* (Princeton: Princeton University Press, 1980).
6. Susan Suleiman, "Introduction," in Suleiman and Crosman, *Reader in the Text*, pp. 23–25.
7. George Bornstein, *Transformations of Romanticism in Yeats, Eliot, and Stevens* (Chicago: University of Chicago Press, 1976), pp. 194–99.
8. Marjorie Perloff, *The Poetics of Indeterminacy: Rimbaud to Cage* (Princeton: Princeton University Press, 1981).

CHAPTER ONE. THE TRANSPARENT LYRIC

1. M. H. Abrams, *Natural Supernaturalism: Tradition and Revolution in Romantic Literature* (New York: Norton, 1971), pp. 199–200.
2. Percy Bysshe Shelley, *Complete Works*, edited by Roger Ingpen and Walter E. Peck (London: Julian Editions, 1926–1929), IX, 340.
3. Samuel Taylor Coleridge, *Biographia Literaria*, edited by J. Shawcross (Oxford: Clarendon Press, 1907), II, 254–55, 258.

4. John Keats, *Letters of John Keats*, edited by Robert Gittings (New York: Oxford University Press, 1970), p. 157.

5. Ibid., p. 38.

6. See M. H. Abrams, *The Mirror and the Lamp: Romantic Theory and the Critical Tradition* (New York: Oxford University Press, 1953), p. 347 n. 77.

7. Robert Pinsky, *The Situation of Poetry* (Princeton: Princeton University Press, 1976), p. 49.

8. Robert Langbaum, *The Poetry of Experience: The Dramatic Monologue in Modern Literary Tradition* (1957; rpt. New York: Norton, 1963); Frank Kermode, *Romantic Image* (1957; rpt. New York: Vintage, 1964); Harold Bloom, *The Anxiety of Influence: A Theory of Poetry* (New York: Oxford University Press, 1973), and subsequent books. See also David Thorburn and Geoffrey Hartman, eds., *Romanticisms: Vistas, Instances, Continuities* (Ithaca: Cornell University Press, 1973), and George Bornstein, ed., *Romantic and Modern: Revaluations of Literary Tradition* (Pittsburgh: University of Pittsburgh Press, 1977).

9. See Bloom, *Anxiety of Influence*, p. 28.

10. Karsten Harries, "Metaphor and Transcendence," *Critical Inquiry* 5 (1978), 76.

11. Robert Langbaum, "New Modes of Characterization in *The Waste Land*," in *Eliot in His Time*, edited by A. Walton Litz (Princeton: Princeton University Press, 1973), p. 109.

12. For a useful taxonomy of this term see W. Daniel Wilson, "Readers in Texts," *PMLA* 96 (1981), 848-63.

13. Marjorie Perloff, *The Poetics of Indeterminacy: Rimbaud to Cage* (Princeton: Princeton University Press, 1981), p. 17. Like Perloff, I am fully aware of the degree to which I depart here from Derridean theory.

14. Ralph W. Rader, "The Dramatic Monologue and Related Lyric Forms," *Critical Inquiry* 3 (1976), 131, 143.

15. Years later Florence Williams claimed that her husband had not in fact attended the Armory Show, but given his interest in modern painting and his frequent visits to New York galleries, this seems highly unlikely, as Paul Mariani suggests in his *William Carlos Williams: A New World Naked* (New York: McGraw-Hill, 1981), pp. 106-107.

16. Considerable attention has been paid to the influence of modern painting on the two poets. See Robert Buttel, *Wallace Stevens: The*

Making of Harmonium (Princeton: Princeton University Press, 1967), especially pp. 148-68; Michel Benamou, *Wallace Stevens and the Symbolist Imagination* (Princeton: Princeton University Press, 1972), especially pp. 1-24; Bram Dijkstra, *The Hieroglyphics of a New Speech: Cubism, Stieglitz, and the Early Poetry of William Carlos Williams* (Princeton: Princeton University Press, 1969); Dickran Tashjian, *William Carlos Williams and the American Scene* (Berkeley and Los Angeles: University of California Press, 1978); Henry M. Sayre, "Ready-mades and Other Measures: The Poetics of Marcel Duchamp and William Carlos Williams," *Journal of Modern Literature* 8 (1980), 3-22; and Peter Schmidt, "Some Versions of Modernist Pastoral: Williams and the Precisionists," *Contemporary Literature* 21 (1980), 383-406.

17. Perloff, *Poetics of Indeterminacy*, pp. 33-34.

18. Schmidt, "Some Versions of Modernist Pastoral," p. 387.

19. Benamou, *Wallace Stevens*, p. 21.

20. James E. Breslin, *William Carlos Williams: An American Artist* (New York: Oxford University Press, 1970), p. 58.

21. Quoted in Perloff, *Poetics of Indeterminacy*, p. 119.

22. Benamou, *Wallace Stevens*, p. 72.

23. Buttel, *Wallace Stevens*, p. 166.

24. Louis L. Martz, "Wallace Stevens: The World as Meditation," in *Wallace Stevens: A Collection of Critical Essays*, edited by Marie Borroff (Englewood Cliffs, N.J.: Prentice-Hall, 1963), p. 148.

25. Ibid., pp. 134, 147.

26. Denis Donoghue, *Connoisseurs of Chaos: Ideas of Order in Modern American Poetry* (London: Faber, 1965), p. 190.

27. Frank Doggett, *Stevens' Poetry of Thought* (Baltimore: Johns Hopkins Press, 1966), p. 192.

28. Donoghue, *Connoisseurs of Chaos*, p. 190.

29. Doggett, *Stevens' Poetry of Thought*, p. 192.

30. Donoghue, *Connoisseurs of Chaos*, p. 210.

31. Merle E. Brown, *Wallace Stevens: The Poem as Act* (Detroit: Wayne State University Press, 1970), p. 68.

32. Donoghue, *Connoisseurs of Chaos*, p. 210.

33. Richard Allen Blessing, *Wallace Stevens' "Whole Harmonium"* (Syracuse: Syracuse University Press, 1970), pp. 125-26.

34. Ibid., p. 126.

35. Joseph N. Riddel, Jr., *The Clairvoyant Eye: The Poetry and*

Poetics of Wallace Stevens (Baton Rouge: Louisiana State University Press, 1965), p. 153.

36. Ibid., p. 155.

37. Alan Perlis, *Wallace Stevens: A World of Transforming Shapes* (Lewisburg, Pa.: Bucknell University Press, 1976), p. 47. For a reading of the poem much closer to my own, see Thomas J. Hines, *The Later Poetry of Wallace Stevens* (Lewisburg, Pa.: Bucknell University Press, 1976), pp. 95–99.

38. Blessing, *Wallace Stevens' "Whole Harmonium,"* p. 70.

CHAPTER TWO. THE THEATER AND THE BOOK

1. Two recent exceptions: William C. Stephenson and Warwick Wadlington, " 'Deep Within the Reader's Eye' with Wallace Stevens," *Wallace Stevens Journal* 2 (Fall 1978), 21–33, and Robert DeMaria, Jr., " 'The Thinker as Reader': The Figure of the Reader in the Writing of Wallace Stevens," *Genre* 12 (1979), 243–68.

2. Merle Brown's *Wallace Stevens: The Poem as Act* (Detroit: Wayne State University Press, 1970), for example, is primarily concerned not with the act of reading, but the act of writing: "A poem is a human act of self-translation, of translating the dark current of feelings into translucent gems. . . . If the poet has translated his feeling far enough, a reader can work his way back through its ritualized forms to its savage center, to the most elemental feeling the poet has of life itself" (pp. 14, 17).

3. Harold Bloom, *Wallace Stevens: The Poems of Our Climate* (Ithaca: Cornell University Press, 1977), pp. 377, 376.

4. R. P. Blackmur, *Form and Value in Modern Poetry* (Garden City, N.Y.: Doubleday, 1957), pp. 200, 201, 211. It should be noted that Blackmur was speaking here only of the *Harmonium* poems.

5. Randall Jarrell, *The Third Book of Criticism* (New York: Farrar, Straus, 1969), p. 63.

6. Hugh Kenner, *A Homemade World: The American Modernist Writers* (New York: Knopf, 1975), pp. 74–75, 78.

7. Jarrell, *Third Book*, pp. 63–64.

8. Robert Langbaum, *The Poetry of Experience: The Dramatic Monologue in Modern Literary Tradition* (1957; rpt. New York: Norton, 1963), p. 182.

9. Ibid., p. 56.

10. George Santayana, *Scepticism and Animal Faith* (New York: Scribner's, 1923), p. 53.

11. Frank Doggett, *Stevens' Poetry of Thought* (Baltimore: Johns Hopkins Press, 1966), p. 87.

12. Richard Allen Blessing, *Wallace Stevens' "Whole Harmonium"* (Syracuse: Syracuse University Press, 1970), p. 81. See also Doggett, *Stevens' Poetry of Thought*, pp. 64–65.

13. Frank Lentricchia, *The Gaiety of Language: An Essay on the Radical Poetics of W. B. Yeats and Wallace Stevens* (Berkeley and Los Angeles: University of California Press, 1968), p. 173.

14. Isabel G. MacCaffrey, "A Point of Central Arrival: Stevens' *The Rock*," *English Literary History* 40 (1973), 606–33.

15. See Doggett, *Stevens' Poetry of Thought*, pp. 71–72.

16. Ibid., p. 81.

17. Helen Hennessey Vendler, *On Extended Wings: Wallace Stevens' Longer Poems* (Cambridge: Harvard University Press, 1969), p. 54.

18. Randall Jarrell, *The Anchor Book of Stories* (Garden City, N.Y.: Doubleday, 1958), p. xx.

19. James Baird, *The Dome and the Rock: Structure in the Poetry of Wallace Stevens* (Baltimore: Johns Hopkins Press, 1968), p. 214.

CHAPTER THREE. THE MOTIVE FOR METAPHOR

1. Louis L. Martz, "Wallace Stevens: The World as Meditation," in *Wallace Stevens: A Collection of Critical Essays*, edited by Marie Borroff (Englewood Cliffs, N.J.: Prentice-Hall, 1963), p. 149.

2. Joseph N. Riddel, Jr., *The Clairvoyant Eye: The Poetry and Poetics of Wallace Stevens* (Baton Rouge: Louisiana State University Press, 1965), p. 27.

3. Percy Bysshe Shelley, *Shelley's Prose*, edited by David Lee Clark (Albuquerque: University of New Mexico Press, 1954), pp. 278–79.

4. Suzanne Juhasz, *Metaphor and the Poetry of Williams, Pound, and Stevens* (Lewisburg, Pa.: Bucknell University Press, 1974), p. 133.

5. Roy Harvey Pearce, "Wallace Stevens: The Last Lesson of the Master," in *The Act of the Mind*, edited by Roy Harvey Pearce and J. Hillis Miller (Baltimore: Johns Hopkins Press, 1965), p. 126.

6. Ibid.

7. In a later essay, Pearce seems to have moved closer to this position: "Decreation is no longer just a stage or a state to be, however unflinchingly, taken into account. Now it has become a

state or a stage to be worked through. On the way to what end? To authentic creation as in fact realization, recreation." Roy Harvey Pearce, "Toward Decreation: Stevens and the 'Theory of Poetry,' " in Frank Doggett and Robert Buttel, eds., *Wallace Stevens: A Celebration* (Princeton: Princeton University Press, 1980), p. 292.

8. Helen Regueiro, *The Limits of Imagination: Wordsworth, Yeats, and Stevens* (Ithaca: Cornell University Press, 1976), p. 179.

9. Riddel, *Clairvoyant Eye*, pp. 166–67.

10. Regueiro, *Limits of Imagination*, p. 183.

11. Ibid.

12. Riddel, *Clairvoyant Eye*, p. 233.

13. Cf. Regueiro, *Limits of Imagination*, p. 203.

14. Frank Lentricchia, *The Gaiety of Language: An Essay on the Radical Poetics of W. B. Yeats and Wallace Stevens* (Berkeley and Los Angeles: University of California Press, 1968), pp. 136, 175.

15. Ibid., pp. 133–34.

16. Helen Hennessey Vendler, *On Extended Wings: Wallace Stevens' Longer Poems* (Cambridge: Harvard University Press, 1969), p. 16.

17. Ibid., p. 132.

18. Ibid., pp. 27–28, 24.

19. Ibid., pp. 18, 25.

20. Ibid., pp. 20–21.

21. Harold Bloom, *Wallace Stevens: The Poems of Our Climate* (Ithaca: Cornell University Press, 1977), p. 211.

22. For a discussion of what Jonathan Holden calls the "blurred-you" in contemporary poetry, see his *The Rhetoric of the Contemporary Lyric* (Bloomington: Indiana University Press, 1980), pp. 38–56.

23. Regueiro, *Limits of Imagination*, p. 180.

24. Cf. ibid., p. 179: "Instead of finding in metaphor a generation of reality, the poet sees 'metaphor as degeneration' (*CP*, 444), always altering the object and undermining the possible experience." See also J. Hillis Miller, *Poets of Reality* (Cambridge: Harvard University Press, 1965), p. 245. For an excellent discussion of the poem, see Thomas J. Hines, *The Later Poetry of Wallace Stevens* (Lewisburg, Pa.: Bucknell University Press, 1976), pp. 254–58.

CHAPTER FOUR. THE NOTHING THAT IS

1. Joseph N. Riddel, Jr., *The Clairvoyant Eye: The Poetry and Poetics of Wallace Stevens* (Baton Rouge: Louisiana State University Press, 1965), p. 225.

2. Roy Harvey Pearce, *The Continuity of American Poetry* (Princeton: Princeton University Press, 1961), p. 408.

3. Randall Jarrell, *The Third Book of Criticism* (New York: Farrar, Straus, 1969), p. 64.

4. See, for example, Marjorie Perloff, "Irony in Wallace Stevens' *The Rock*," *American Literature* 36 (1964), 327-42; Isabel G. MacCaffrey, "A Point of Central Arrival: Stevens' *The Rock*," *English Literary History* 40 (1973), 606-33; Thomas J. Hines, *The Later Poetry of Wallace Stevens* (Lewisburg, Pa.: Bucknell University Press, 1976); Harold Bloom, *Wallace Stevens: The Poems of Our Climate* (Ithaca: Cornell University Press, 1977), pp. 253-374; and Robert Buttel, " 'Knowledge on the Edges of Oblivion': Stevens' Late Poems," *Wallace Stevens Journal* 5 (1981), 11-16.

5. Pearce, *Continuity*, p. 413.

6. Riddel, *Clairvoyant Eye*, pp. 225-26.

7. Helen Hennessey Vendler, *On Extended Wings: Wallace Stevens' Longer Poems* (Cambridge: Harvard University Press, 1969), p. 270.

8. Ibid., p. 269.

9. Ibid., p. 66.

10. Merle E. Brown, *Wallace Stevens: The Poem as Act* (Detroit: Wayne State University Press, 1970), p. 179.

11. Ibid., p. 176.

12. Bloom, *Wallace Stevens*, p. 275.

13. Riddel, *Clairvoyant Eye*, p. 233.

14. Vendler, *On Extended Wings*, p. 271. Harold Bloom's response anticipates mine: "There is much harshness, yes, but a great deal also that is rather more genial than is usual in Stevens. There is some deprivation, and yet the flesh, the sun, the earth, and the moon are all there, and so are a surprising vigor and joy" (*Wallace Stevens*, p. 306).

15. Vendler, *On Extended Wings*, p. 6.

CHAPTER FIVE. MACHINES MADE OF WORDS

1. Hugh Kenner, *A Homemade World: The American Modernist Writers* (New York: Knopf, 1975), p. 81.

2. Joseph N. Riddel, Jr., *The Clairvoyant Eye: The Poetry and Poetics of Wallace Stevens* (Baton Rouge: Louisiana State University Press, 1965), p. 14.

3. Denis Donoghue, "Williams, a Redeeming Language," in his

The Ordinary Universe: Soundings in Modern Literature (New York: Macmillan, 1968), pp. 181-82.

4. Riddel, Clairvoyant Eye, p. 12.

5. William Carlos Williams, "Owl's Clover" (review of The Man with the Blue Guitar), The New Republic 93 (November 17, 1937), 50.

6. William Carlos Williams, "Comment: Wallace Stevens," Poetry 87 (January 1956), 235-36.

7. William Carlos Williams, "Notes from a Talk on Poetry," Poetry 14 (July 1919), 213.

8. Roy Harvey Pearce, The Continuity of American Poetry (Princeton: Princeton University Press, 1961), p. 339.

9. Rod Townley, The Early Poetry of William Carlos Williams (Ithaca: Cornell University Press, 1975), pp. 152-53.

10. J. Hillis Miller, "Williams' Spring and All and the Progress of Poetry," Daedalus 99 (1970), 421.

11. Cf. J. Hillis Miller: "Williams gives himself up in despair and establishes a self beyond personality, a self coextensive with the universe. Words, things, people, and God vanish as separate entities and everything becomes a unit. . . . The personality of the poet is obliterated in a total adhesion of the mind to the object in its actuality." Poets of Reality (Cambridge: Harvard University Press, 1965), pp. 291, 347.

12. Neil Myers, "William Carlos Williams' Spring and All," Modern Language Quarterly 26 (1965), 300. See also James Breslin, William Carlos Williams: An American Artist (New York: Oxford University Press, 1970), pp. 54-55.

13. First complete draft, dated 5/23/44, of Williams' "Commentary" to his translation of Quevado's The Dog and the Fever, p. 19 (Yale American Literature Collection), as quoted in Linda Welsheimer Wagner, The Poems of William Carlos Williams (Middletown, Conn.: Wesleyan University Press, 1964), p. 60.

14. See for example Wagner, Poems of William Carlos Williams, pp. 53-74, and Suzanne Juhasz, Metaphor and the Poetry of Williams, Pound, and Stevens (Lewisburg, Pa.: Bucknell University Press, 1974).

15. William Carlos Williams, "Letter to an Australian Editor," Briarcliff Quarterly 3 (October 1946), 208.

16. Juhasz, Metaphor, pp. 13-14.

17. William Carlos Williams, unpublished letter dated 5/29/43

(Yale Collection), as quoted in Wagner, *Poems of William Carlos Williams*, p. 110.

18. William Carlos Williams, notebook entry dated 10/18/50 (Yale Collection), as quoted in Townley, *Early Poetry*, p. 117.

19. Thomas R. Whitaker, *William Carlos Williams* (New York: Twayne, 1968), p. 33. See also Hugh Kenner, *The Pound Era* (Berkeley and Los Angeles: University of California Press, 1971), pp. 397-404, and his *Homemade World*, pp. 57-90.

20. Whitaker, *William Carlos Williams*, p. 17.

21. Miller, *Poets of Reality*, pp. 299, 300.

22. Breslin, *William Carlos Williams*, pp. 53-54.

23. Pearce, *Continuity*, p. 341.

24. Breslin, *William Carlos Williams*, p. 73.

25. Alex Preminger, ed., *Princeton Encyclopedia of Poetry and Poetics* (Princeton: Princeton University Press, 1974), p. 582.

26. William Carlos Williams, "A New Collection of Modern Poetry" (Yale Collection), as quoted in James Guimond, *The Art of William Carlos Williams* (Urbana: University of Illinois Press, 1968), pp. 100-101.

CHAPTER SIX. ONLY THE DANCE

1. Marjorie Perloff, *The Poetics of Indeterminacy: Rimbaud to Cage* (Princeton: Princeton University Press, 1981), p. 151.

2. James Breslin, *William Carlos Williams: An American Artist* (New York: Oxford University Press, 1970), p. 203.

3. Linda Welsheimer Wagner, *The Poems of William Carlos Williams* (Middletown, Conn.: Wesleyan University Press, 1964), p. 126.

4. Thomas R. Whitaker, *William Carlos Williams* (New York: Twayne, 1968), p. 152.

5. Breslin, *William Carlos Williams*, p. 211.

6. Ibid.

7. See for example SL, pp. 296-97 and 313-14.

8. Paul Mariani, *William Carlos Williams: A New World Naked* (New York: McGraw-Hill, 1981), p. 670.

9. Breslin, *William Carlos Williams*, p. 213.

10. Wagner, *Poems of William Carlos Williams*, p. 119.

11. Paul Mariani is a notable exception. In his discussion of the last poems he emphasizes "a renewed cinematographic sense. . . . Present the curve of a moment, catch that and let the reader imagine

the rest. . . . Now in these late poems he provided a new emotional complex which included the reaction of the observer brought into the field of the poem itself" (*William Carlos Williams*, p. 726).

12. Whitaker, *William Carlos Williams*, p. 152.

13. As "The Red Wheelbarrow" could not. See Hugh Kenner, *A Homemade World: The American Modernist Writers* (New York: Knopf, 1975), pp. 59-60.

POSTSCRIPT

1. (Amherst: University of Massachusetts Press, 1981). Further references will be included in the text.

2. Charles Altieri, "The Poem as Act: A Way to Reconcile Presentational and Mimetic Theories," *Iowa Review* 6 (Summer-Fall 1975), 108. For related investigations see his "Objective Image and Act of Mind in Modern Poetry," *PMLA* 91 (1976), 101-14; "Presence and Reference in a Literary Text: The Example of Williams' 'This Is Just to Say,' " *Critical Inquiry* 5 (1979), 489-510; and *Enlarging the Temple: New Directions in American Poetry During the 1960s* (Lewisburg, Pa.: Bucknell University Press, 1979).

3. Ralph J. Mills, Jr., *Cry of the Human: Essays on Contemporary American Poetry* (Urbana: University of Illinois Press, 1975), pp. 7-8.

4. Harold Bloom, "John Ashbery: The Charity of the Hard Moments," in *Contemporary Poetry in America: Essays and Interviews*, edited by Robert Boyers (New York: Schocken, 1974), p. 117.

5. *The Guardian* (April 19, 1975), p. 8.

6. Bloom, "John Ashbery," p. 127.

7. Louis A. Osti, "The Craft of John Ashbery: An Interview," *Confrontation*, No. 9 (Fall 1974), 87.

8. Bloom, "John Ashbery," p. 118.

9. Interview by Anna Quindlen, *New York Post* (February 7, 1976).

10. John Ashbery, *Houseboat Days* (New York: Penguin, 1977), p. 21.

11. For a brilliant discussion of this strategy in other Ashbery poems, see Marjorie Perloff, *The Poetics of Indeterminacy: Rimbaud to Cage* (Princeton: Princeton University Press, 1981), pp. 248-87.

12. Ashbery, *Houseboat Days*, pp. 45-46.

Index

LIBRARY OF CONGRESS CATALOGING IN PUBLICATION DATA

Walker, David L., 1950-
The transparent lyric.

Includes bibliographical references and index.
1. American poetry—20th century—History and criticism.
2. Stevens, Wallace, 1879-1955—Criticism and interpretation.
3. Williams, William Carlos, 1883-1963—
Criticism and interpretation.
I. Title.
PS324.W34 1984   811'.5209   84-1986
ISBN 0-691-06606-X